In Search of
MY FATHER

PAT TRAVIS EATHERLY

To Ted + Vee —
My square dance
friends.

Best Wishes
+
God Bless You
Pat Travis Eatherly
4-16-87

BROADMAN PRESS
Nashville, Tennessee

© Copyright 1987 • Broadman Press
All rights reserved
4257-27
ISBN: 0-8054-5727-5
Dewey Decimal Classification: B
Subject Headings: EATHERLY, PAT TRAVIS //
TRAVIS, MERLE
Library of Congress Catalog Number: 86-31752
Printed in the United States of America

Library of Congress Cataloging-in-Publication Data

Eatherly, Pat Travis, 1939-
    In search of my father.

    1. Travis, Merle. 2. Eatherly, Pat Travis,
1939-   . 3. Country musicians—United States—
Biography. I. Title.
ML420.E18A3 1987   784.5'2'00924 [B]   86-31752
ISBN 0-8054-5727-5

Dedication

To *Gene Eatherly*, my husband, whom I love and respect for his devotion to God and our family, *Dawn*, *Paige*, and *Tricia*

In Memory of
Mary and *Merle*, my parents whom I love with all my heart

With Appreciation to
Claudia Martin, *Sue Hilburn*, and *Mickey Dowdy* . . . without their listening ears, words of encouragement, and expert critiquing, this book could not have become a reality; to Mary Brite who taught me to call myself a "writer" at her Brite School of Christian Writing; and to the staff of Broadman Press who suggested a deeper search, bringing hidden truths to the surface.

Foreword

About three months before Merle Travis' death he and I took a memorable journey to Drakesboro, Kentucky. The purpose of the trip was to visit Mose Rager, a legendary guitar finger picker and one of Merle's early mentors. Neither of us had seen Mose for some time, and he was terminally ill.

I called to pick up Merle and his wife, Dorothy, at John Hartford's guest house in East Nashville. Dorothy advised that she would not be going because "you fellows should have a chance to talk."

Drakesboro, the hometown of Mose Rager and Ike Everly (father of the Everly Brothers), is about ninety miles from Nashville, if one takes the shortest and most scenic route. And it's close to Merle's birthplace, Rosewood. The road is narrow and winding most of the way. We stopped a few miles south of Drakesboro and visited Patty's aunt and Merle's sister, Vada. Merle mentioned before we got to her house that she would be smiling and said that she had been smiling all her life. She was smiling and was very glad to see us. The home was very neat with pictures of Merle, his brothers, and his father hanging on the walls. I studied the photo of the father closely. It was of 1920 vintage and showed a dapper fellow in a sporty hat. I noticed he had bright, intelligent eyes.

Vada taught Merle to read and write before he started school, and it was obvious that he was one of her favorite brothers. After visiting her for a spell we journeyed on to Drakesboro and the home of Mose and Laverda Rager. There was a lot of reminiscing by Mose and Merle, and the guitar was passed around. Their playing still had that magic sound I remembered hearing when I was fifteen. I had decided years ago that Mose and Merle are more alike than brothers. They had identical mannerisms, always laughing after every guitar lick and never taking life or themselves seriously. This was about the third time the three of us had been together, and I think we all realized it would probably be the last. Pictures were taken right at sunset, good-byes were said, and we pointed the car toward Nashville.

It was fun visiting Mose, Laverda, and Merle's sister, but equally nice was the conversation Dorothy thought we should have. There were a lot of truths given to one another and for no one else's ears, such interesting things as Merle's telling me of following Mose and Ike around when he was a child, listening to them play, and then rushing home to try and imitate what he had heard . . . of Clayton McMichen's band playing Drakesboro out of WHAS, Louisville (a very young friend saw the show, and the friend kept insisting that Merle go backstage and play a tune for them) . . . of the fiddler, Carl Cottner, being so impressed that he pestered McMichen until he hired Merle a few weeks later (they were a little late in finding Merle, though, because of the 1937 flood which caused so much damage in the Ohio and Mississippi Valley areas; they finally found him on high ground in Evansville, Indiana) . . . of moving to Los Angeles from Cincinnati because Smiley Burnette told him, "I'd rather be poor and live in LA than rich and live somewhere else" . . . of writing "Smoke, Smoke, Smoke (That Cigarette)" while painting a fence . . . of visiting a girlfriend on his motorcycle, stopping under a street light on the way home, and writing on scrap paper words to "Dark As a Dungeon."

In fact, he wrote some of the greatest songs of his career during that period because he was doing a folk song album for Capitol, didn't have enough material, and Lee Gilette, the record executive, told him to go write some folk songs. He informed Lee that folk songs are supposed to be old, handed down from generation to generation, etc. Well, among the "new folk songs" were "Sixteen Tons," "Dark As a Dungeon," and others which are on their way to becoming some of our richest musical heritage.

Merle and I were close from our very first meeting in 1945. And there were many other visits and conversations. I remember how proud he was of Patty when she was winning beauty contests, and I was with him and remember his happiness when she was named "Kentucky Derby Queen." Merle was one of the very clever ones and, as I said to a reporter when Merle left us, "Merle Travis could write you a hit song and sing it; he could draw you a cartoon; play you a great guitar solo; or he could fix your watch." I miss him greatly and am thankful for this opportunity to tell you about him.

As the years go by I feel certain the world will want to know more and more about this highly creative man, Merle Travis. Patty's autobiography helps fill that need because it covers a lot of interesting areas in his life that even I never knew. Perhaps you will find Patty's search for her father to be as interesting as I did.

—CHET ATKINS

Merle Travis was a friend of mine, and I loved him for many years.

He taught me a lot; how to shoot, throw a knife, whittle, and other arts and crafts, but mainly he taught me to respect myself as one of God's creations.

His music lives in my heart. From time to time I'll sing his songs.

The legend that was Merle Travis was all-American, a man of love, compassion, and humility.

My life is richer because I knew him.

—JOHNNY CASH

In Search of My Father is a good book by Pat Travis Eatherly. It could figure importantly in research if they ever make a picture of Merle Travis's life. Lord knows he had a colorful, exciting, interesting, at times sad, and successful one.

I first met "Trav" when we worked at the same radio station, KXLA, in Pasadena, California, towards the late 40s—I as an announcer, he as a featured performer with "Cliffie Stone's Dinner-Bell Roundup" gang, a daily country-western variety show. I really wasn't a singer then, but I used to go into their studio and sing bass with their quartet during the Gospel segment of the program.

Subsequently we did years of personal appearances and radio and television together with Cliffie. It was during this time Merle married his second wife, the girl singer on the show, Judy Hayden. So, I didn't know his first wife and only met "Patty," then a little girl, when she visited California. Trav was one of my dearest friends whose talents I admired tremendously.

If only he could have read this book before passing on. He would have been so pleased to know that "everything turned out real good." I'm sure he never wanted or planned to be estranged from his first little girl. It just happened that way. Geographically he was so far away and in the prime of his career. I'm sure there wasn't time in the day to wind his watch. Mary and Patty happened so early in his life. He was just a teenager. His "life" really started "after Mary and Patty."

"Know me as I am, love me if you will, hate me if you must" . . . is true Travis. He was a wonderful writer. Songs, letters, poems were among many other things he did exceptionally well. I know, his "Sixteen Tons" was the best thing that ever happened to me. And, wow! Wait till you read his letter to Pat of October 29, 1980. That's real Travis writing.

Merle Travis will always be special to me. As a special tribute to the man, I have framed several obituaries of his, each in its own way telling of a different Merle Travis. One I read often is entitled "Merle Travis—Farewell to a Legend" by Rich Kienzle in *Country Music* magazine. A real tribute to the man.

Someday, when I'm taking time to smell the roses, I'm going to Ebenezer, Kentucky, and stand by my good friend's bronze plaque and relive some of the good memories of days gone by.

—TENNESSEE ERNIE FORD

Hardly a day goes by that I or Ramona don't hear or say something that is associated with Merle Travis. What a mind that man had.

I guess it was when I came to WLW in 1941, to take an audition, that I first met Merle. We "hit it off" right away, as he was raised only about forty miles from where I was raised. Our folks said and did the same things.

We hunted and fished together, we made the first record that King Records released and called ourselves "The Shepard Brothers," named after a little cartoon of a man I used to draw.

We got together with Alton and Rabon Delmore and formed the "Brown's Ferry Four Quartet." Alton taught us to read shaped notes. Merle learned a lot quicker than I did.

We had a lot of fun riding the "Boone County Jamboree" bus that we nicknamed the "Galloping Goose." We sang and picked all the way to personal appearances.

After Merle went to California he wrote the big hit "Smoke, Smoke, Smoke (That Cigarette)." Before that I said one day, "Merle, sometime I wish you would write me a song against cigarettes!" He knew how I hated them; he said "OK, I will sometime." That afternoon he called and said, "I've got your song ready." And as usual it was a good one. I recorded it and sang it on a lot of personal appearances.

If someone needed a song, he was always willing to oblige. He knew I liked the cartoons he drew, and nearly every letter I got from him would have a cartoon drawing on it.

I am really proud that he included me as one of his many, many friends.

—GRANDPA JONES

Every parent and child should read *In Search of My Father*. This searching, poignant, real-life story reveals the deep need to love, communicate, and care between father and child. Merle Travis was a gifted musician and songwriter but suffered for many years the loss of a fulfilling father-child relationship.

Pat Eatherly found it, after much unhappiness, in a real relationship with her Heavenly Father, which is the ultimate fulfillment for each of us. Because of her Christian commitment, Merle Travis finally found his daughter.

Pat Eatherly has been painfully honest in this account. May God honor her obedience.

—DALE EVANS ROGERS

Contents

1

"My Dad's a Movie Star"

Clutching my quarter, I tiptoed to push my money through the glass hole to exchange it for a movie ticket. *Galloping Thunder* was playing at the Hollywood Theater for the Saturday matinee, and I knew I'd have a chance to see my daddy. I stopped by the glass show case to read: "Charles Starrett as The Durango Kid, Smiley Burnette, the West's number-one comic in *Galloping Thunder* with Merle Travis and his Bronco Busters—a Columbia Picture."

"Hurry, Patty," my best friend, Reda Ann Brown, called to me as I stood gazing at the publicity pictures. The music had already started.

We hurried down the aisle to the front row. If we sat near the back, the boys in the balcony would throw popcorn or gum on our heads. Today we didn't want to be disturbed.

People all over Kentucky were proud of my dad. The name, Merle Travis, had brought a lot of attention to his home state of Kentucky since he had written "Smoke! Smoke! Smoke! (That Cigarette)." Tex Williams's recording of it was Capitol Records' first million seller. Certainly everyone in Morgantown, Kentucky (population 500), knew him. He was a songwriter, musician, and movie star—and he was my daddy!

When he and Mom divorced he moved to California, and I didn't see him often. Occasionally I would receive a letter from him about the excitement going on in Hollywood, and almost always there would be an 8 x 10 black-and-white glossy picture for my scrapbook. Each picture was autographed especially to me, such as, "To my sweetheart, Patty: with all my love, Dad—

Merle Travis," or sometimes simply signed "From your Pappy."

If my obsession with the devotion toward my father ever caused Mother any anguish, she never expressed it. Mother always encouraged my collection of mementos. I know it was hard for her to find a job and support us after their divorce, especially after her second marriage didn't work either. That's why I was living with her parents, my Pa and Ma Johnson.

Grandpa was a coal miner during the week and a preacher on the weekends. Even though he didn't approve of "worldly," sinful picture shows, I was allowed to go.

The lights dimmed and darkness closed out reality. *Galloping Thunder* began. Finally, the moment I'd been waiting for arrived. A tall, handsome cowboy stepped forward. His dark eyes sparkled as he tilted his white Western hat back, propped his foot on a chair, placed his guitar on his knee, and began to sing. A closeup filled the screen with my dad.

His gentle eyes appeared to be looking into mine. Was that knowing little grin just for me?

My make-believe world lasted only two hours; then it was over. Reda Ann and I made our way through the noisy crowd to face the dazzling daylight. From the corner of my eye, I saw a little girl pointing at me. "There she is," I overheard her loud whisper. "Ain't she lucky?"

Yes, I am lucky, I thought proudly. My friend and I held hands to cross the street to the courthouse square. Grandpa was sitting under a giant shade tree deep in conversation with some other old men. He waved for us to join him. We sat nearby watching a group of boys in overalls shoot a game of marbles until Grandpa was ready to go.

Our old black sedan kicked up a cloud of dust as we traveled the fifteen-mile stretch of gravel road to South Hill. It gave Reda Ann and me time to talk and giggle about our day in town. We had felt so special dressed alike in our red-and-white-gingham peasant dresses gathered at the neck with black grosgrain ribbon. Sometimes Grandma made clothes for me on her treadle sewing machine out of fabric she'd saved from feed sacks, but today we were in store-bought dresses. The wind tossed my friend's long finger curls. I envied her naturally curly hair. Grandma tried to finger-curl my hair, but it was never as pretty as Reda's.

Life in South Hill, Kentucky, was like a page out of the past. There was no electricity, no running water, and simply no modern conveniences. There was a pot-bellied stove in the front room, where we burned coal, a galvanized tub brought in for bathing, always plenty of good food to eat, and kinfolks to keep us company.

Cooking, canning, quilting, and scrubbing clothes on a washboard were a natural way of life. Fortunately, I was young enough to remember all this as fun. When I entered third grade, we exchanged our coal-oil lamps for electric ones, but the well up the road remained our source of water.

The summer before beginning the fifth grade, I moved fifty miles away to Owensboro, Kentucky (population 33,000), with my mother. She was now working on an assembly line for Ken-Rad Lamp Corporation, which later became General Electric Tube Plant. We rented two rooms in a lady's house near Mom's work. That year, Longfellow Elementary School was difficult for me, but I managed to pass the fifth grade with the encouragement of Mrs. Ehresman, my favorite teacher.

I kept the fantasy of my famous father alive with my bulging scrapbook. Dad remarried a glamorous professional singer whose stage name was Judy Hayden. Her pictures were added to my collection. She began to write now instead of Dad. On October 8, 1949, a baby daughter, Merlene Roberta Travis, was born. I received an announcement with this note inside.

Dear Patty,

We thought you might like to know our new little girl is your half-sister, and we've been told by people who

knew you when you were a baby, that she looks an awful
lot like you did.
    Your daddy sends love and kisses and will write real
soon.

Love,

    June

I was so excited I could hardly think or talk about anything
else. I had a sister. My dream for the next two years was to visit
my father and meet this new little sister. Mother was in favor
of my idea and helped make arrangements for me to visit California the summer of 1951.
    The nearest airport of any size was thirty-five miles away,
across the Ohio River, in Evansville, Indiana. Mother and I
often visited Dad's older brother, Uncle Taylor, and his wife,
Aunt May, who lived in Evansville. They had three daughters,
Polly, Peggy, and Barbara. Peggy and Polly were married but
lived in the neighborhood. Their family was exceptionally close.
Mother and I always felt welcome in their home. I enjoyed
hearing the story about Uncle Taylor who hand built Dad's first
guitar. Dad joked that his first guitar was "Taylor made"! We
loved this family, and they eagerly helped us make reservations
for me to fly out of their town.
    When the scheduled date arrived, I excitedly watched the big
DC-3 appear at the Eastern Airline departure gate. The bold
letters on its side read, "The Great Silver Fleet." The two big
props nearly blew my starched crocheted hat off. Aunt May had
made it for me to complete my new navy blue suit. I just knew
I looked older than twelve. Even though this was my first flight,
I assured Mother I would be fine. She snapped my picture as
I boarded the steps and waved good-bye.
    Flying through the white fluffy clouds made my ears pop.
Looking down, the city of Evansville became a miniature town
and then disappeared.

After many hours of flying my racing heart began to calm. I tried to imagine what it would be like to stay in my father's home with his new wife and baby. My visits with him had only been brief, when he was playing a show nearby. Now, I would actually be living with him in his house! Unable to analyze my emotions, I sighed deeply and glued myself to the window. The sprawling city of Los Angeles illuminated the darkness. Lights glittered as far as I could see, like a giant Christmas tree. The stewardess tapped me on the shoulder, smiled, and reminded me to buckle my seat belt for landing. Again my heart pounded with excitement.

When the door opened, and the steps were rolled up to the plane, I spotted Dad right away. He ran over to me and wrapped me in his arms.

"Hi, Honey, how was your flight?"

"Oh, Daddy, it was so exciting, and the stewardess was so nice, and when I grow up that's what I want to be." I hardly caught a breath as I chattered nervously.

"Honey, this is June, your stepmother."

She smiled and hugged me. "We're so glad you're going to be with us for the summer."

"Thank you," I smiled sheepishly. I studied June and became painfully aware of my appearance. By now my navy suit was wrinkled and filled with lint. My white blouse was tea-stained from spilling when we hit an air pocket. June's long blond hair was curly, her clothes were fresh and neat, and her makeup was more theatrical than I was used to, but her brown eyes were friendly and warm. I liked her.

"Where's Merlene?" I questioned.

"Oh, she's at home with a babysitter. It's a long ride to the San Fernando Valley from the airport, and we didn't want her to be tired and cranky for her big sister," June laughed.

After claiming my luggage, we walked through the Los Angeles Airport to Dad's car. He opened the trunk and tucked my suitcase inside. I approvingly observed the shiny two-toned Lincoln Cosmopolitan, complete with clean, wide white-wall tires. I felt proud to be riding in style. *This is going to be a great summer,* I thought.

2

Summer in San Fernando Valley

Andy Devine, the famous Western comedian who spoke in that unique raspy squeal of a voice, donated his private home and pool to the city of Van Nuys. It was now a popular neighborhood swimming center for the San Fernando Valley. Dad immediately signed me up for swimming lessons.

"Honey, you'll be swimming like Esther Williams before the summer is over," he predicted.

Swimming became my favorite pastime. Soon June trusted Merlene to go with me. She was only two, but she loved the water. Merlene got so suntanned that she looked like the Coppertone Baby advertisement. Dad teased us about being from south of the border!

Merlene was a pudgy little cherub. She would mimic anything she was told to and constantly made me smile. It was amazing how she could recognize Dad's guitar music when she heard him on the radio. Once when the disc jockey played his well-known instrumental of "I'll See You in My Dreams," Merlene announced in her most possessive baby voice, "My daddy!" Of course, she was right.

Curling up in front of the black-and-white television was a special treat for me, since few people I knew had a set. Merlene would snuggle beside me to watch my favorite program, "The Little Rascals." When the program was over, she'd gesture with her chubby arms bent and palms upward and say, "Ah gone." One habit I'll never forget was how she'd suck her middle two fingers freeing her index finger to pick her nose!

Sometimes it seemed awkward having a full-time daddy. I

wasn't used to a man in the house. My insecurity told on me one morning when I rode to the grocery with Dad. Glancing at him in the car, I noticed his pants were unzipped. I squirmed and squirmed, trying to get the courage to tell him, but simply couldn't. Getting out of the car he noticed and quickly adjusted his zipper.

He quizzically looked at me in amazement and asked, "Patty, weren't you going to tell me?" He only had to look at my crimson face to find his answer!

Slowly, I began to feel more comfortable being a member of this family.

June and Dad had a thirty-minute television program on KECA TV called "Merle Travis and Company." I felt very important riding into Hollywood with them for early-morning rehearsals and then watching the show. Roaming the American Broadcasting Company's studio was exciting. There was an especially interesting set for a program called "Space Patrol." It was complete with a rocket ship and a miniature town on a huge table. The cameramen and sound equipment made it come alive as space ships zoomed in and out. They were actually dangling from an overhead string manipulated by the special-effects man.

Jerry Colonna, a bug-eyed comedian with a villain-like mustache and a huge gap between his teeth, was in a studio nearby. I'd sneak over often and watch his show. This hilarious entertainer delighted his audience with his rare vocal ranges. He usually ended every song on a very high note. So high, I was tempted to put my fingers in my ears!

I observed everything on the sets, from the makeup artists to the movie stars. Dad would often complain about the heavy makeup he had to wear.

"It's just like working in the mines," he chuckled. "The only difference is the color."

I'd laugh remembering how Pa Johnson looked coming home from the coal mines back in Kentucky.

Most of Dad's show was singing and playing the guitar, but one portion allowed him to demonstrate his artistic ability. While Dad listened, June read a letter from a fan describing a person in detail. He would spontaneously draw them in cartoon style. This drawing was mailed to that fan.

"Patty, I'm going to teach you how to draw a simple caricature and let you do it on the show," he promised.

After much persuasion and much practice ahead of time, I agreed. Of course, I was to pretend this was the first time I'd ever heard the letter. With a thick black artist's pen and white paper on a giant easel, I rigidly forced the lines as Dad had rehearsed me.

"This man has a long nose and a sharp pointed chin," Dad instructed.

I thought I was doing fine, but before he could finish reading I completed my picture with the oversized ears and thick, bushy flattop. That was the beginning and end of my television career!

"Patty, I'll bet you've never been deep-sea fishing, have you?" Dad questioned. "Remember my friend, Tennesse Ernie (Ford)?"

Of course, I remembered him. I'd seen him lots of times on Cliffie Stone's "Dinnerbell Roundup." Tennesse Ernie was that funny man who wore overalls, blacked his tooth, and talked real country. Once I saw him all dressed up in a suit and pink shirt with French cuffs and shiny gold cuff links, and I was surprised how handsome he was.

"Ol' Ern and some other buddies are going deep-sea fishing, and I'm taking you along," Dad continued.

He turned to June and added, "You ain't never seen better fishermen than the Johnsons. Why, Patty's uncles back in Kentucky can outfish anybody."

Then he'd tell some fishing story about one of Mother's six brothers. They did hunt and fish a lot, but Dad made them sound so important. I felt proud when he talked like that.

"You orta hear Arley on the mandolin," he kept bragging about my uncle. "B. W. ain't bad on the guitar either."

"Patty, who does this remind you of?" Dad rared back his head, threw out his chin, and with a little grunt, cleared his throat, and started singing in full volume,

> On a hill far away
> stood an old rugged cross,
> The emblem of suffering and shame;
> And I love that old cross
> where the dearest and best
> For a world of lost sinners was slain.[1]

"That's Pa Johnson," I exclaimed. "You sound just like him." Dad could imitate anybody.

The fishing trip proved to be profitable for me aside from my becoming sunburned and seasick. Everyone on the boat put in a dollar, and the one who caught the biggest fish won the jackpot. I begged Dad not to put any money in for me since it was my first time, but he insisted, saying it was "just luck." I won the $20 jackpot! Tennessee Ernie patted me on the back and said, "Congratulations, Gal, you must take after your kinfolks I've heard so much about."

June and Dad planned another memorable excursion for us to the San Bernardino Mountains at Big Bear Lake. June outfitted me with a pair of red leather cowboy boots, a suede, fringed jacket, and plaid Western shirt to go horseback riding. Dad added the finishing touch by tying a bright red scarf around my neck. I don't think this costume improved my riding skills, but it did boost my enthusiasm.

The summer soon slipped away and it was time for my return to Kentucky. June took me shopping before I left and, among other things, we bought two blue parakeets. I named them outstandingly original names—Blue Boy and Blue Girl. We schemed to smuggle them back on the plane without getting caught. I would simply carry them in a tiny cage in a hatbox with holes poked in it. Nobody would ever know.

Flying back, the stewardess offered to take my hatbox. "Oh no, thank you," I responded, clutching it protectively. I hoped she hadn't noticed my anxiousness.

At one point during the flight I relaxed with my head back, thinking about all the things I had to tell Mother. She would want to hear about it all. My thoughts were interrupted when I heard a bird chirping. Forgetting about my parakeets, I peered out the window. Then I remembered. Quickly, I grabbed my jacket and covered the hatbox, hoping no one else heard them.

Leaning back again I began wondering what the school year would be like. I would be entering the seventh grade at Central Junior High School. Mother and I had moved in with a lady named Theda Kitchens, whose husband was killed in World War II. She had a daughter my age named Shirley. We lived in Theda's small two-bedroom home on Twenty-Seventh Street. All the white stucco houses on that street were identical except for different-colored shutters. Ours were red. Mother and I shared one of the bedrooms. Although I imagined how nice it would be to have a room of my own, at least living in a house was better than the rooms we had been renting.

Shirley and I had our disagreements, but we managed to get along most of the time. I thought she was spoiled and vice versa. Perhaps our mothers tried too hard to compensate for our need of fathers.

Too bad Mom's marriage to that Fort Knox soldier didn't work, I thought. He promised to buy me a horse and move us to Wyoming, but their marriage didn't last long enough even to move away from Theda's. On weekends he would come from Fort Knox to see Mother, but their plans never did materialize.

All I knew was: he was insanely jealous and accused Mother of some terrible things after they married. I learned later that, once in a fit of temper, he rummaged through her old photographs, and if he found one of Mother and Dad together, he took the scissors and cut the portion of Dad out of the picture. Mom even had to go to the doctor because she broke out in red hives. The doctor diagnosed it as nerves. I was relieved when their divorce was final, and he no longer came around. Mother had shared precious little about this with me. She had explained it was best we stayed where we were and didn't move. I was glad, too. I would be happy to see her when the plane landed. I began to realize how much I'd missed her, but I also realized how much I was going to miss Dad, June, and my new baby sister.

NOTE

1. Words by George Bennard, 1913. Copyright 1913 by George Bennard. © Copyright Renewed 1941 (extended), The Rodeheaver Co. Used by permission of Word Music, Inc.

3
Another New Daddy

Why did I cry every time I passed a mirror? I couldn't bear to look at myself. *How can I face school tomorrow looking like this? Especially entering junior high school.* Mom had emphasized it would look just like the picture on the Toni permanent box. She had painstakingly rolled each section of hair on those tiny plastic pink rods while I impatiently endured the awful stench. I had done my part by handing her a new piece of tissue for each curl. *And now look at me! I'm ruined.*

"Patty, don't be so upset. It'll loosen up. It's just tight because it's a new permanent," Mother tried to assure me.

"It's kinky and fuzzy and ugly," I pouted. "It's so short my ears show. I hate it. I'll never get another Toni." I stomped off to sulk.

Why did I have to have big ears? I fumed. *"It's a Travis trait,"* I was told. *Well, that's one thing I wished I hadn't inherited from Dad.* Usually I was proud when people told me I looked exactly like him. My round face and brown hair and eyes were all right, but I was constantly self-conscious about my very big ears. Nobody ever claimed I looked like my mother. Her eyes were blue, and her hair was golden blond—natural, too. Sometimes people asked what she used to bleach her hair. The question always aggravated her. Once she made up a wild story for a lady who refused to believe her color was natural. Mother thought it was next to sinful to change the color of one's hair. As a matter of fact, she never worked hard at being pretty—she simply was.

At thirteen, I'd already outgrown her five-feet-four-inch

frame by two-and-a-half inches. My shoe size also surpassed
hers by two sizes. Many times I'd hear people remark, "You
sure are a big girl for your age." I dreaded being one of the
tallest in my class. *It wouldn't be so bad if the boys weren't so
short,* I'd often fret.

Soon the anxiety of entering Central Junior High lessened,
my permanent loosened, and I became comfortable with my
new routine. When the school bell signaled us to change classes,
I learned to charge through the wide hallways with the stam-
pede of students. Hall monitors guarded the aged, wide, sagging
stairs to remind us not to go in the wrong direction. They
threatened to carry our names to the office if we failed to obey.

History had never been my favorite subject, but I became
excited hearing my teacher talk about leaving class early to see
General Eisenhower. "Class, we are very fortunate that our
school is so close to the railroad track," she announced. "Tomorrow Dwight D. Eisenhower will make a whistle stop right
here in Owensboro, Kentucky. He is campaigning for the 1952
Republican nomination for president of the United States."
Then she handed out "I Like Ike" posters.

When Mother came home from work, I showed her my
poster. "Look, Mom, this man could be the next president of
the United States," I informed her.

"Hang onto that poster, because if the Republicans get in
office, we may need it to paper our walls!" Mother responded.

Her remark made no sense to me. *She must not like Ike,* I
thought. Of course, what I didn't understand was her fear of
another depression which had been blamed on the Republicans.
Her memory of World War II which ended in 1945 was still
vivid. She sometimes talked about the days when such things
as women's hose, sugar, and tires were rationed. Also I'd heard
how the war had put many unskilled women to work in facto-
ries. Mom's first job had been sewing in a parachute factory.
Now under President Harry Truman the nation was peaceful
and prospering.

Oh well, who cares? I thought. *Tomorrow we're going to get out of history class early.* That was the best part.

Soon the school year was over with few exciting events. There was one drastic change at home, however—the new man in Mother's life. He was called by his last name, "Jones." When it came time for Mother to sign my eighth-grade report card, Jones would be her new name, too. Maybe I would learn to like him, but he was so old-fashioned. He wore his short, curly hair parted in the middle and criticized my dirty white buckskin shoes. Didn't everyone know that was the style? Even his car was old and ugly, but Mother pointed out it was always clean. I guessed being clean and quiet were his outstanding qualities.

We moved from Theda's to an upstairs apartment within walking distance of school. An extended area of the apartment which was part of the attic served as my room. Mother bought some red-and-gray plaid material and made a bedspread and a skirt to tack around a small wooden table which served as a dresser. My rollaway bed had a white leather Hollywood headboard, and now there was room to leave it open all the time. Finally, I could claim a room of my own.

Now I could invite my best friend, Peggy Quinn, over to spend the night. I also loved staying at her house. She had the whole upstairs for her room. Often we'd stay up until late into the night searching through stacks of movie magazines for our favorite stars. Peggy was wild about Tony Curtis, and I'd fallen for John Derek. We'd carefully cut out their 8 x 10 color pictures to frame. When Mrs. Quinn would tell us for the last time to turn off the lights, we'd frantically grab a handful of bobby pins and curl our hair in the dark.

Peggy was an only child born to her parents late in life. Mr. and Mrs. Quinn adored her and gave her many privileges. If the gang needed a ride to the movies or the roller-skating rink, Mrs. Quinn was always available. Kids flocked to her house.

It was easy to be friends with Peggy. She seemed so happy all the time and had such an outgoing personality. She had a knack for drawing people to her. When a joke was told, she laughed the hardest. When there was a ball game, she cheered the loudest. Her clothes were the latest, including cashmere sweaters and Capezio shoes. She and I shared our lives and our secrets.

"Peggy, have you ever been to California?" I asked.

"No, but I have an aunt who lives out there in a town called Anaheim. Wouldn't it be fun if we could go together some-time?"

Now we shared the secret desire to go to California.

We mustered up the courage to ask our mothers. Of course, since I'd already been once, I felt I was an expert on travel, and there was nothing to it. "Nothing except a great deal of ex-pense," we were reminded. To save on the cost, Peggy and I agreed we would be willing to take the train instead of flying. Mrs. Quinn suggested she and my mother drive us as far as St. Louis, Missouri, so we wouldn't have to make any changes.

Plans were set, and we were en route to sunny Southern California.

It'll really be fun this time with a friend along, I thought. However, the train seemed so slow compared to my last trip. I wondered if we'd ever make it there. Mother had said we could enjoy the scenery; but as far as I was concerned this was boring. St. Louis had been boring, too. We'd spent an extra day sightseeing. *Why had Peggy made that remark about the way I acted there anyway? She kind of made me mad.* I wasn't inter-ested in St. Louis, but she thought I should have acted like it to please our mothers.

I suppose Peggy knew me as well as any friend I ever had. I'll never forget when she wanted to visit the country with me. In a way I was ashamed of living like I did in South Hill with my grandparents. I asked Mother about taking Peggy with us some weekend, and she thought it was a good idea. "You have nothing to be ashamed of because our people are poor," Mom pointed out. "Besides, they're honest and they're clean." Then she added a thought I'll never forget. "Patty, don't ever judge a person for what they have but for what they are."

I glanced over at Peggy who was curled up sleeping to the constant sway of the moving train. Laughing to myself, I remembered Bobby chasing her down the road with a pig's tail. Hog-killing season was just over, and leave it to Bobby to tease Peggy like that! She ran from him screaming at the top of her lungs. Bobby was Mom's baby brother. He was only two months younger than me, so I never called him "uncle."

Peggy and I remained friends even after our trip to the country, so I guess Mother was right. There was one thing I'd never told Peggy. Actually, I'd never told anyone. It was the day I'd walked home from school to our upstairs apartment and found it empty. Jones often sarcastically threatened to leave when he and Mother had a disagreement. This time he did. When I opened the door that day, even the furniture was gone. The emptiness I experienced still haunted me. When Mom came home from work, I was still sitting in a stupor in the middle of our empty living room.

"It'll be all right," Mother assured me. We'll work it out," she reassured me, putting her arm around my shoulder as she hugged me close to her.

She and Jones worked it out by making up and moving into a trailer home on Triplett Street. Mother explained that this would be more like living in our very own home. Unfortunately that remedy failed, and so did the marriage.

The train slowed with a jerk, jolting me back into the present.

"Where are we?" Peggy asked.

"I don't know, but I'll be glad when we get to California," I admitted. "This is taking forever."

"Oh, just think of the fun we're going to have," Peggy brightened optimistically. "We're going to Hollywood to see all the movie stars, to the beach, and that amusement park called Knott's Berry Farm, and you'll get to play with Merlene and your newest little sister, Cindy."

June had told me all about the new baby in a letter. She wrote that Cindy didn't smile as much as Merlene, and Dad had nicknamed her "The Sad-Faced Comic." *Yes,* I thought, *now I have two half-sisters which will make it twice as hard to leave!*

4

Facing Change

"Patty, hurry and get up. You're going to be late for school."

I peeked through the covers to see Mother dressed for work. She had to leave before me. The old house we were renting was so cold in the mornings. The high ceilings and the windows that reached nearly to the floor made for an impossible draft.

I rolled over, burying my head in my pillow, procrastinating, when I heard a familar sound of voices from the people renting the other half of the house. "You're trying to kill me! Someone help!"

"There goes Mr. _____ again," I observed matter-of-factly.

"Yes, poor old thing; he doesn't know what he's saying," Mother responded with sincere compassion.

"Well, I don't see how Mrs. _____ puts up with that crazy old man. I don't care if he is her husband."

"Now, Patty," Mother reminded me, "Mrs. _____ loved him through the good years, and she is devoted to taking care of him through the hard times. We know his accusations aren't true."

Every time Mrs. _____ brought him something to eat, he accused her of trying to poison him. *How could she have the patience to put up with the old goat?* I wondered.

"There are some biscuits in the oven," Mother interrupted my thoughts. "Just leave the oven door down when you go to school, and it'll warm up in here." She grabbed her purse and rushed off to work.

I forced my warm body up. My bare feet hit the cold hard-

wood floor. I snatched my clothes from the closet and raced to
the bathroom to dress. It would be warm in there with the gas
heater turned up full blast.

As soon as I finished dressing, I heard my ride outside honking. *At least he won't have to wait for me today,* I thought
proudly. *I'll make the bed when I get home.* It was nice to have
a ride to school in the mornings, even if I did usually walk
home. I rushed from the back of the house in the kitchen,
through the bedroom, and picked up my books off the coffee
table in the front room. My friend was impatiently honking
again.

"I'm coming, I'm coming," I yelled, running across the wide,
sprawling cement porch.

Owensboro Senior High School afforded many new adven-
tures my freshman year. The "Red Devil" football team was
one of the best in the state of Kentucky, and all I could think
about was becoming a cheerleader for the team. I was terribly
disappointed when I tried out and didn't make it. I couldn't
wait to try the following year.

School was dismissed early after a pep rally. The spirit was
high as we yelled to the top of our lungs, "We're going to
B-E-A-T Paducah!" I envied the cheerleaders in their white
skirts lined with red satin, topped with red sweaters and a big
black "O" on the front for Owensboro. All six girls wore black-
and-white saddle oxfords with bobby socks. That's what I wanted more than all else.

Kids darted out through the wide double doors, yelling playfully to one another. Tugging at my coat, I braved the chilling
November winds. I wished someone would give me a ride, but
they didn't. If I walked at a brisk pace, it would take only thirty
minutes to get home.

I turned up my coat collar to ward off the cold and discovered a hole in my pocket when I tried to warm my hand while
balancing my books with my free hand. *I hate this old coat,* I
sulked. I wanted a new one but Mother declared she couldn't

afford it. Many of the girls at school had cuddly mouton coats, and I longed for one. Mother suggested I write my father and ask for a coat. *Well, maybe I would.*

Turning the corner off Frederica, Walnut Street was in sight. That big old porch looked welcome. I skipped up the three steps, searched for the key hidden in the mailbox to hurry inside. A familiar letterhead caught my attention. It was Dad's stationery marked MERLE TRAVIS boldly across the top, designed with a cactus at the beginning and end of his name.

I juggled my books on my knee as I turned the key. As soon as I was inside, I dropped my books, plopped down in the nearest chair, and tore into the envelope. I discovered a letter from my stepmother, June.

November 17, 1953

Dearest Patty,

Don't faint, I'm finally writing. No sense making excuses, I know, but just to keep you up on things I'll tell you what keeps me so busy. For one thing I fly to San Francisco every week to do a TV show. Wednesday is shot getting ready to go; Thursday I go do the show and come back Friday beat! Saturday your dad and I work together at Town Hall Party in Compton which includes an hour radio show and a two-hour TV show. Getting in so late (or should I say early?) messes up what Sunday is left, and Monday and Tuesday I try to catch up on what I got behind in.

In between the other things I try to stay acquainted with the babies and learn the crazy tunes they throw at me to do every week. Of course, your dad is on the go as usual, and the ride from here to Compton on Saturdays is almost our only time together.

Her letter ended by asking what I wanted for Christmas and then added, "Dad sends his love, and he'll write when he can."

She always promised that, but he never wrote anymore. He

was so busy keeping up with the demands of show business he
had no time for other matters. A chill raced over my body. Was
it the temperature or an inkling that something was going
wrong with Dad's marriage? With a bit more clear thinking and
less naïvete, I could have read between the lines to predict
another inevitable divorce.

I jumped up, pushing hidden fears away, and headed for the
kitchen. Even it was cold. *I wonder why? Didn't Mother leave
the gas oven on? The stove door was wide open, but no warmth.
Maybe it's not lit. Where did Mother keep our matches? There
they are; on top of the refrigerator.* "Sunny California," I yelled
out loud. "Why can't I be there now?"

Mother had warned me about the dangers of gas. She'd
always been the one to light the stove and the gas heater in the
bathroom. I'd watched her many times. There really wasn't
anything to it. Merely turn the knob, and don't leave it on too
long before striking the match. Carefully I reached for the oven
knob as I promptly struck the match. Simultaneously a thunderous explosion knocked me off my feet, and a sudden swoosh
of blue flames leaped from the mouth of the oven. I was startled
and scared. My heart began racing and my face felt as though
it were on fire. I looked about the room, and there were no
flames. My hands quickly examined my hair, my face, and my
clothing. *No flames. Thank God. But why is my face so hot?*
Anxiously, I hurried to a mirror. My hair, eyebrows, and
eyelashes were singed. Maybe I could cover the redness with
makeup.

Oh, I look awful, I worried, studying my face. *I'll never be
the same. What will the kids at school think of me?* My appearance had become extremely important. Mother often com-
plained about my primping too much. *Oh, no, what is Mother
going to say?* It was almost time for her to be home from work.

When she came in, I was still at the mirror trying to conceal
the evidence of my accident. She immediately sensed something
was wrong. "Patty, what happened?"

I began explaining. She quickly analyzed the situation and suggested that more than likely the pilot light had gone out on the oven, causing the blue flames when I tried to light it. She checked to see if I'd turned the gas off. I had.

"I'm thankful you weren't burned, Patty," Mother sighed with relief.

"Well, I look ugly enough with my hair singed, and my eyebrows and eyelashes nearly gone," I whined.

"Patty," Mother reprimanded my vanity, "be grateful God spared you, and stop worrying so much about how you look!"

She just doesn't understand, I pouted.

5
When the Glitter Is Gone

As we rode through the streets of Peoria, Illinois, a giant billboard advertising Gene Autry's Western Variety Show caught my attention.

"My father is playing in the Gene Autry Show," I informed my taxi driver as he drove us from the airport to the hotel where Dad would meet me.

"Is that right?" he grunted, unimpressed.

Undaunted by his negative response, I chattered. "It's going to be a wonderful show. Gail Davis, the star of television's "Annie Oakley" series, is going to be there and also that funny comedian, Pat Buttram. Have you ever heard of them?"

"Everybody's heard of them," he answered nonchalantly. "What's your father do in the show?"

"He sings and plays the guitar."

"Yeah, what's his name?"

"Merle Travis," I answered in my most important tone.

"Merle who?"

"Merle Travis. Surely you've heard of his songs, 'Smoke! Smoke! Smoke! (That Cigarette),' 'Nine Pound Hammer,' 'So Round, So Firm, So Fully Packed,' and 'Divorce Me C.O.D.' "

"Yeah, yeah, now I know who you're talking about," he admitted, pulling in front of the hotel. "Here you are, young lady. Enjoy your stay in Peoria."

"Thanks." I paid him, pulled out my suitcase, and he drove away.

Walking up to the hotel desk, I set my suitcase down and

inquired about the room number for Merle Travis. "He's in room 413," the smiling clerk answered. "You his daughter?"

"Yes sir, I am."

"He left word for you to meet him in the dining room down the hall and to your left. You can leave your suitcase here."

"Thank you, sir." I quickly turned and headed down the long corridor. I was thrilled Mother had let me come. Dad would be here only for a one-night show, so this was one of those rare occasions I'd get to be with him, even if it was for such a short time.

I stopped at the entrance of the restaurant, and the hostess walked over to me. "I'm supposed to meet my father here," I said, feeling a little shaky. *What if he isn't here?* I thought, searching the room. At that moment, Dad's eyes caught mine. He hurried over, gave me a big hug, and ushered me to his table.

"Patty, I want you to meet a performer from the show."

I glanced down to see a very pretty, petite lady smiling at me.

"This is Audrey Haas, one of the country's outstanding contortionists."

"One of the country's what?" I quizzed. Until now I had felt so grown up for my fifteen years.

Dad laughed, putting me at ease. "She's an acrobatic dancer, Honey. Wait till you see her tonight. She can nearly turn herself inside out!"

Dad was right. Audrey Haas was incredible to watch. She twisted into the most impossible positions imaginable. Yet she did it with the poise and balance of a ballerina.

I was entranced with the entire show. Annie Oakley strutted out on stage in her fringed white leather vest and skirt, then demonstrated her marksmanship. Her beautiful blond hair was braided in two long pigtails tied with white satin ribbons to match her blouse. Then came a square dance group called The Promenaders, followed by The Strong Family. The Strongs were listed in my souvenir program as America's leading rope, whip, and juggling artists, along with Lindy, their trick dog.

Finally the curtains closed, and I heard the amplified voice of the announcer, "Ladies and gentlemen, tonight we have one of the country's foremost authorities on folk songs, and one of the world's finest guitar pickers, straight from the hills of Kentucky to the hearts of people everywhere. Let me introduce Merle Travis!"

As the curtain opened, I heard the familiar sound of Dad's guitar. The audience applauded. After his instrumental number, he introduced his next song. "I never will forget one time when I was on a little visit down home in Ebenezer, Kentucky," Dad recalled. My ears perked up, and I strained to listen. Ebenezer was just down the road from where Pa and Ma Johnson lived.

Dad went on in his natural, easy style. "I was a-talkin' to an old friend of the family who had known me since the day I was born. He said, 'Son, you don't know how lucky you are to have a nice job like you've got and don't have to dig out a livin' from under these hills and hollers like me and your pappy used to.'

"When I asked him why he never had left and tried some other kind of work, he said, 'naw sir, you jest won't do that. If'n ever you get this ol' coal dust in your blood, you're jest goin' be a plain ol' coal miner as long as you live.'

"He went on to say, 'It's like a habit, sort of like chewin' tobaccer.'"

Then Dad played an introduction on his guitar and started singing "Dark As a Dungeon."

> Come and listen you fellows, so young and so fine,
> And seek not your fortune in a dark dreary mine.
> It will form as a habit and seep in your soul,
> 'Till the stream of your blood runs as black as the coal.

And then the chorus

> It's dark as a dungeon and damp as the dew,
> Where the danger is double and the pleasures are few,
> Where the rain never falls and the sun never shines,
> It's dark as a dungeon way down in the mines.

As I listened, I wondered if that's how it was for Grandpa Johnson. I'd never been inside a coal mine. I'd never given much thought about what it was really like.

Dad continued singing:

> It's a many a man I have seen in my day,
> Who lived just to labor his whole life away,
> Like a fiend with his dope and a drunkard his wine,
> A man will have lust for the lure of the mine.
>
> I hope when I'm gone and the ages shall roll
> My body will blacken and turn into coal,
> Then I'll look from the door of my heavenly home,
> And pity the miner a-digging my bones.

Dad's song ended with the chorus:

> Where it's dark as a dungeon and damp as the dew,
> Where the danger is double and the pleasures are few,
> Where the rain never falls and the sun never shines,
> It's dark as a dungeon way down in the mines.[2]

For the remainder of his performance, Dad captivated the audience with his good-natured country stories and songs. They were obviously delighted, and so was I.

Of course, to climax the show, Gene Autry came riding in on his horse, Champion. Thunderous applause echoed through the building as he sang, "I'm Back in the Saddle Again," his theme song.

Comedian Pat Buttram appeared on stage in his fringed suede jacket and turned-up floppy cowboy hat calling, "Mr. Artery (sic)." Just the sound of his gravelly voice produced a contagious wave of laughter. The show ended on a happy note when the whole gang squeezed onto stage to take a final bow.

As the crowd was leaving, I made it backstage. The policeman guarding the entrance from the gathering fans let me through. I was relieved I'd been introduced to him earlier.

Dad, still dressed in his costume, was packing up his guitar and amplifier. "Is that a Nudie suit?" I asked.

"Yep, sure is. They're easy to spot, huh, Patty?"

I had become accustomed to Nudie's famous tailoring. He used loads of sequins. Dad's Western-cut suit had a guitar design on each side of the front and one on the back with MERLE TRAVIS printed down the neck of the guitar.

"Hey there, gal," I heard a raspy voice behind me. When I turned around, I saw Pat Buttram. "I jest want to make your acquaintance; any daughter of my ol' buddy, Trav, is a friend of mine."

"Oh, hello, Mr. Buttram. I sure did enjoy the show."

"Well, I'm mighty proud to hear that. Jest what did you like the very best?"

I thought for a moment and remembered The Strong Family with their cute dog Lindy. "I think my favorite was the act with the dog in it."

Mr. Buttram and Dad looked at each other and laughed. Then Dad made a comment I've always remembered. "Little children and trained animals will steal the show every time."

I was even enjoying watching the cast busily packing up to leave. There still was a lingering crowd of fans outside the backstage door. One young boy tried desperately to grab Mr. Autry's attention. "Hey, Gene," he yelled. "Hey, Gene."

Finally Gene Autry turned around and looked at him. The young boy had this disappointed look on his face and remarked, "Yea, I didn't know you were so fat!"

I couldn't help but snicker. Mr. Autry pretended he didn't hear.

Pretending was an important part of show business, I was learning. Soon the stage was stripped of sets and lights, and the glitter was gone. The show would be packed up, and the performers would become passengers on giant tour buses to start over in a new town.

Dad had made arrangements for me to ride on the bus with him to the outskirts of town. That way I'd get to be with him a little longer. A hotel near the airport was where the bus driver would let me off. Some people might have thought I was too young to spend the night in a hotel alone, but Dad felt I was a big girl and could handle it.

Soon the exhausted cast was crammed into the bus and we were heading out. I sat in a seat next to the window and watched the lights of Peoria fade away. There was practically no traffic at that hour of the morning. A low whisper hummed through the stillness in the bus. I studied Dad's profile in the dim shadow of light. He looked weary. *Poor Dad,* I thought. He had told me about the breakup between him and June. There hadn't been much time for private conversation, but then I wasn't good at talking to Dad about such personal matters anyway. I wondered if I'd ever be with Merlene and Cindy again. I closed my eyes tightly to hold back the tears. *It's over,* I told myself. *I'll get over it.*

Slowly the bus came to a stop. Dad pulled my suitcase down from the overhead rack. "Well, Patty, reckon this is where you and I part. I'm sure proud you came to be with your ol' Pappy tonight. Be careful and have a safe flight home. Don't forget to write."

I forced a brave smile as we hugged. A few sleepy heads bobbed up to wave good-bye as I stepped off the bus into the night. Clutching my suitcase, I strained to see Dad's face in the window where we'd been sitting together, but I couldn't. Somehow my strength drained from my body as I watched the loaded bus pull away. I could see the flickering neon hotel sign through the drizzling rain. It wasn't far to walk from the corner, but suddenly I didn't feel as brave as I had before. The town was eerily silent, and I could hear the echo of my steps. I hastened my pace. *Why was I thinking this way? I'm a big girl. I can handle it. Hadn't Dad said so?* Taking a renewed grip on my suitcase and my emotions, I rushed toward the hotel until I was safe inside the warm lobby.

"May I help you?" I heard an old man's voice behind a worn, wooden registration desk.

"Yes, sir, I need a room for the night. I'll be flying from your airport in the morning. I'm going home to Kentucky. Can I get a cab from here?"

The old man nodded his head in the affirmative.

"Will you please ring my room with a wake-up call at eight o'clock?"

Let's see. Had I remembered everything Dad had told me? The old man nodded to a rather tired-looking attendant dressed in a shabby uniform to show me to my room. I followed him into the elevator. He pushed number five, and I watched as we passed floors two, three, four, and finally arrived at number five.

I trailed behind him down the hall where he unlocked the door to my room. Cautiously entering, I observed my sleeping quarters as he switched on the light. There was one bare light bulb dangling from the ceiling of the room. He placed my suitcase on a worn luggage rack and shifted his weight from side to side, staring at me. *Why doesn't he leave?* I began to worry. With more experience I would have realized he was waiting for a tip. Finally he left, and I locked and bolted my door with the chain.

It's silly to be scared, I thought. *After all, I'm almost sixteen.* Quickly I changed for bed. Pulling the chain to turn out the light, I crawled between the cool sheets and pulled the cover securely around my chin. A stream of light shone across my dark room from an open transom above my door. A red blinking light from an all-night restaurant across the street cast strange shadows on the walls. *I'm OK,* I consoled myself. *I'll be safe at home in my own bed tomorrow night.* After giving myself a pep talk, I forced my eyes closed, and sleep gradually came.

NOTE

6

Secret Revealed

I stood in a dark corner, refusing to dance, as I watched the crowd at Teen Town. Ernie Ford's record was turned up full volume as he belted out the words to "Sixteen Tons" in his deep baritone voice:

> Some people say a man is made out of mud,
> A poor man's made out of muscle and blood,
> Muscle and blood, skin and bones
> A mind that's weak and a back that's strong.
>
> You load sixteen tons, and what do you get?
> Another day older and deeper in debt
> Saint Peter, don't you call me 'cause I can't go,
> I owe my soul to the company store.[3]

The YMCA offered the high school kids a fun night once a week, and I always looked forward to participating—but not tonight. Early in the fall when Ernie Ford recorded my dad's song, "Sixteen Tons," I was jubilant. I watched it climb to the top of the *Hit Parade.* The lively, finger-snapping tune was constantly on the radio. Merle Travis was once again in the limelight. There seemed to be more publicity for the songwriter than for the singer. At least that was true in Kentucky, but that publicity had turned sour overnight.

Everytime I heard Dad's song it reminded me of that awful day, January 4, 1956. It started out as any ordinary Wednesday morning, but the news reached school ahead of me and could not be squelched among the students. Innocently, I learned that

Merle Travis had been arrested. Somehow I found a newspaper and retreated to an empty classroom. I opened it to read:

"16 Tons" Composer in Wild Battle with Wife

My eyes darted to a picture of Bettie, Dad's new wife of only eight months. She was clutching her bathrobe, standing outside their home, with a policeman on each side of her. The caption under the picture read: "Songwriter's wife tells of terror and pistol whipping."

How could this be? I had just spent last summer with Dad and Bettie in California. We'd had a wonderful time with her two sons, Dennie and Mike, my new stepbrothers. Bettie had even arranged a picnic for the whole family, including Merlene and Cindy, at Hollywood's Griffith Park. Julie, a girl my age who lived next door, also went along. All six of us jokingly called thirty-year-old Bettie "Mom." Dad had laughed and teased and had been unusually playful that day. And now this! It must be a mistake.

I read on:

> Merle Travis, cowboy singer and composer of the top hit song, "16 Tons," today surrendered to police an hour and 18 minutes after he barricaded himself in his North Hollywood home with a rifle and a shotgun.
>
> His pretty wife said he had pistol-whipped her and threatened to "kill anyone who comes near the house." She then fled to a neighboring home with her two children by a previous marriage, Mike, 8, and Dennis, 10, and phoned frantically for help.
>
> More than a score of armed officers surrounded the house at 12406 Chandler Boulevard. They used the loudspeaker in an attempt to persuade the singer to drop his guns and walk out of the house.

Tears blurred my vision as I continued:

Travis, 37, was grabbed by police . . .

I couldn't go on. The school bell rang, and students raced to their classes. Numbly, I folded the paper and laid my head on the desk. I was thankful this room wasn't used for first period. I knew I'd be late to class, but I didn't care. I was startled by someone's hand on my shoulder. I looked up into the compassionate eyes of Mrs. Carpenter, a science teacher.

"Patty," she soothed me, almost in a whisper. "I read all about what happened with your father, and I want you to know I'm very sorry."

I tried to speak, but nothing came out. After a few moments of silence, she reached into her pocket and offered me a tissue.

"Thanks," I mumbled, wiping my wet cheeks.

Mrs. Carpenter sat down beside me. "Patty, don't worry about what other people will say or think. You aren't responsible, and you don't need to apologize for anything. Just hold your head up and pretend nothing ever happened."

I frowned and wondered if that were possible. Shaking my head "yes," as if to indicate obedience to the teacher's advice, I gathered courage to stand up. I still hadn't found my voice, but I was sniffing and swallowing hard to gain control. Suddenly, Mrs. Carpenter added a sentence meant to console me. Instead it infuriated me.

"Patty," she continued, "I understand, because sometimes alcoholics do things when drinking they wouldn't ordinarily do."

An alcoholic? What did that have to do with anything? What made her think my father was an alcoholic? With mixed emotions I gave her a weak smile and walked into the hall to face the day.

Later, the loud music tried to bring me to my surroundings at Teen Town. *Why was I still letting this bother me?* I wondered. *Hadn't Dad explained when I called him that he'd only been kept in jail overnight?* He rationalized how ridiculous and out of proportion the news media made the issue sound. Besides, Bettie wasn't even mad at Dad. She said he didn't mean to hurt her, and he was closer to a nervous breakdown than anything else because he'd been working so hard.

Suddenly a crowd of kids grabbed my hand and dragged me out on the dance floor to join them in the Bunny Hop. As I held onto the person's waist in front of me, I entered into the fun, jumping and shouting, "forward and backward, hop, hop, hop." Soon a whole chain of kids were hopping around the floor until the record ended, and we nearly collapsed with exhaustion.

"Hey, Patty, hurry and get your coat. It's time to go," yelled my friend, Diane Vittitow. Diane and I were both cheerleaders. I secretly admired Diane and was proud to be her friend. Tonight I was spending the night in her home.

"Come on," she coaxed, "we've got a ride home with Ann." Ann Holder was the daughter of Harry Holder, who owned the Ford car dealership, so she always had a new car.

"Are we going to Snyder's Drive-In for something to eat?" I questioned.

"Yeah, why not, I'm starved," Ann answered.

After the crowd met at the restaurant and filled up on milk shakes, French fries, and hamburgers, we reluctantly waved good-bye to the gang and made the rounds home. Ann let Diane and me off in front of her stately brick house on a tree-lined cul-de-sac. Diane's mom and dad greeted us when we came in. "Are you girls hungry?" We looked at each other and laughed.

"I take it that means you filled up at Snyder's," Mr. Vittitow remarked good-naturedly.

I smiled shyly. Diane's father was a prominent figure in Owensboro. His picture and name could be seen on billboards all over town advertising his insurance agency. Everyone knew him as "Chubby," for obvious reasons. He was also the chairman of the school board. Although he was extremely friendly, I felt awkward around him.

After saying good night, Diane and I walked upstairs to her bedroom. "Whoops, be right back, I forgot something," she explained, and darted back down.

I glanced around her beautifully decorated room. *She's so lucky to live in such a nice home and have such nice parents.* Mom had promised me that since she and Lee had married, we would be moving into a house. It was kind of hard becoming used to a stepfather again, but Lee Edwards had become Mother's husband as of December 31, 1955. Having a man around the house again after Mother and I had been alone for almost four years was a big adjustment. He was nothing like Diane's father. Lee was a carpenter from the country, but he seemed to make Mother happy. Wasn't that what counted? *Anyway, if we moved into a house, I could at least have my own room,* I reasoned.

My mind continued to wander as I plopped down on the edge of Diane's bed and stroked the smooth fabric of her blue ruffled bedspread. Then I noticed her open diary on the night stand. Under any other circumstances, I wouldn't have considered reading someone else's diary, but there it was wide open—right in front of my eyes. I looked down and saw my name. This stirred a curiosity that caused me to pick it up and read the short sentence dated January 4, 1956. It read, "Well, tonight Patty's Dad got drunk and beat up his wife."

Hurriedly, I shut the diary. My heart pounded with hurt and anger. I hoped Diane would not guess anything was wrong when she came back upstairs. After all, I knew it was none of my business to be reading her personal diary; and, of course, what she'd written was the truth. But I thought she was my friend. *Why couldn't she have been more understanding?* I made up my mind never to speak a word about this. How could I expect her to understand? I didn't understand myself.

NOTE

7

Untarnished Hero

Sorting through my latest collection of newspaper clippings helped me relive the excitement that was now history. Owensboro's *Messenger–Inquirer* had recorded the event well. I read and reread many of the articles about the "Merle Travis Day" celebration in Ebenezer, Kentucky, on June 29, 1956.

"Friends Pay Tribute to Composer Travis" was the headline of one article, and this one included a picture of me unveiling a monument dedicated to Dad. I read beneath the picture:

> THE UNVEILING—Pat Travis, daughter of Songwriter Merle Travis, Friday afternoon unveiled a monument to the composer of "16 Tons" at "Merle Travis Day" observance in the hamlet of Ebenezer, Kentucky. Pat, of 426 Walnut Street, Owensboro, has herself become famous in this area as a winner of several beauty contests.

Funny, I thought, *how important they even make me sound.* I had entered a contest at the roller-skating rink and had surprisingly won. It led me to win the regional contest for the Roller Skate Rink Operators of America and to place second in the national contest. The next summer I was crowned queen of a local contest as "Miss Game and Fish Association." Dad must have told the reporters about it. He made a big fuss about my winning, like it was really special.

It was interesting to see how creatively the newspaper wrote about the Merle Travis Day. An article by Jack Hudgins read:

> More than 12,000 people invaded this Muhlenberg County community Friday to pay a living tribute to the

area's most popular son—Merle Travis, composer of "16
Tons," as he unveiled a monument the homefolks had
"chipped in" to buy.

Whereas Travis as a miner's son once walked barefoot-
ed in the deep dust of a dirt road, Friday he traveled the
same path in a yellow Cadillac convertible with a chauf-
feur at its wheel.

The mass of humanity liked it. They screamed and
shouted, and rushed at the native son now converted to
the Hollywood set. And Merle liked it too, rising to accept
handshakes from old timers who had worked with his
father, Uncle Rob, at nearby Beech Creek coal mine.

I stopped reading to reminisce about that hot summer day.
Dad had never looked better. He wore a conservative navy
Western suit with a white shirt and red striped tie to match his
red Western boots. His white cowboy hat accentuated his almost black hair and framed his California-tanned face. Bettie
radiated love and admiration for her honored husband. Only
young Dennie and Mike seemed unaware and unimpressed
with the fanfare.

Then I examined the picture of the monument I had unveiled. The inscription under the bronze portrait was inscribed:
"Dedicated to Merle Travis who has done so much toward
directing the spotlight on his home through his writing of folk
songs about his home and his people. His song writing, his
singing, and guitar playing have won the hearts of many, and
the respect of all fellow workers."

I remembered how we walked to that special tin-roofed plat-
form where Dad waved his Stetson hat at the crowd. After we
sat down, the master of ceremonies, Bobby Anderson, began
introducing people who had contributed somehow or another
to the career of Merle Travis. Among the most popular was
Gene Autry, who was dressed in a summer brown Western suit
and white ten-gallon hat. He addressed the crowd and ended his
talk by declaring, "I consider Merle Travis to be one of the

greatest writers of American music in the world today, and I
am glad to count him among my closest friends."

Then Chet Atkins made his appropriate comments. Afterwards, Mr. Anderson called on me. Caught up in the mood of
the whole affair, I heard my voice echo out over the microphone, "This is one of the greatest days in my life. I am bub-
bling over with happiness, and I am very happy for my father."
Dad stood up, gave me a hug, and walked me to my seat.

About a dozen telegrams were read from entertainers who
couldn't be there, such as Tennessee Ernie Ford, Red Foley,
and Pee Wee King. Telegrams were also read from Kentucky's
governor, A. B. (Happy) Chandler, and other important politi-
cal figures. There was even a letter from the the president of the
United States, Dwight D. Eisenhower.

After nearly two hours of vocal tribute, Dad and I were
escorted across the road where a large limestone monument
was to be unveiled. The property had been donated by a lady
named Mrs. Baugh. Dad lovingly called her "Miss Bunnie."
Many years before, Dad had sat on her front porch on this exact
spot listening to hometown musicians, such as Ike Everly and
Mose Rager, play the guitar. He would be influenced by them
forever. Ike's talented sons, Don and Phil (The Everly Brothers), performed for the celebration.

For me the walk across the road was solely for the purpose
of unveiling the monument that stood waiting to be uncovered,
but to Dad I'm sure it represented a brief walk into the past of
his childhood. Even the poignant memory of his parents was
present since their graves were in sight. Laura Etta Travis, my
grandmother, died February 21, 1939, only one month before
I was born, and William Robert Travis died December 20,
1942. I was sure they would have been proud of their son that
day.

Before the unveiling, a four year-old, pint-sized cowboy
stood tall to delight the anxious audience with several verses of
"Sixteen Tons."

You could hear a deep sigh from the almost reverent audience when I finally pulled the cover away to reveal a bronze portrait gleaming in the sunlight. Large letters spelling "Merle Travis" curved overhead. Embossed on one side was a pick and a shovel, and on the other a replica of his guitar. I'll never forget Dad's whispering under his breath so only I could hear, "Look at those ears, Patty; they got 'em life size, didn't they?" It was our private joke, but it made us both smile as the photographers snapped away.

When it was Dad's turn to speak, an air of anticipation swept through the crowd. Every eye approvingly watched him step to the microphone. I spotted Dad's brothers, Uncle Taylor and Uncle John Melvin, in the crowd. Then I noticed the sweet, round face of Dad's sister, my Aunt Vada Adler, smiling proudly at her famous youngest brother. Humbly Dad began by saying, "I didn't write 'Sixteen Tons' . . . you did. Some of you lived it."

He went on, "I hope I will never bring dishonor to this county, community, this group of people. I left here many years ago . . . a poor boy . . . hoping only to find a job. I knew what I wanted but didn't know if I'd get it. I have had some success and am happy. But the happiest part of it all is that I can return and know that all of you are my friends. Otherwise you would not be here."

I remembered how the crowd broke loose with loud and long applause. Dad buried his head in his hands.

If anyone knew or remembered the bad publicity that had swept the news only five months earlier, it was never mentioned. These loyal friends and fans came to honor their hero, and nothing would tarnish their image of Merle Travis.

8

College or Career?

He was tall, blond, and handsome, and everyone was talking about him. He created a new interest at First Baptist Church, especially among the young people. He was charming and outgoing, and had a fantastic sense of humor. He was our new pastor, Dr. Jess Moody.

Dr. Moody's wife, Doris, taught our girls' Sunday School class, and for the first time in a long while, I looked forward to being there. I knew Mother was relieved she no longer had to talk me into going to church on Sunday mornings. Another element of excitement was the Moodys' interest in drama. They had asked me to participate in a new church-sponsored television program on station WFIE called "Contact."

Mrs. Moody wrote skits about circumstances in the home, and they were acted out to the point of the problem which led the situation to the pastor's study for resolution. I was so excited the first time I appeared. My role was that of a dissatisfied housewife. When my husband lost his temper, I was to throw down a dish I was drying, slap his face, and begin to cry. The most difficult part of this scene was slapping the man playing opposite me; but, under the tension of the lights and cameras, I became so involved, I really let him have it! It certainly made for an effective drama and a very realistic handprint on his face. When I threw the dish, the camera zoomed in on the broken pieces, then faded into the pastor's study where Dr. Moody spoke about putting the pieces of an unhappy marriage back together.

As I rode home with the Moodys after the program, we

discussed my college plans. I would soon be graduating with the 1957 senior class of Owensboro High School.

"Patty, have you ever thought about studying drama?" Dr. Moody asked. Before I could answer he continued, "There is a college near Lexington called Georgetown Baptist, where I could possibly get you a drama scholarship. On campus is a group that is traveling to Europe under Professor Corey with their unusual presentation called *The Book of Job.* Just think, you could travel with them and see countries all over the world."

I began to think seriously about his suggestions. *I do enjoy acting. It's one of those pursuits that would please Dad; and Mom would like for me to go to a church school.* Her commitment to the church had recently become important to her.

That fall I enrolled as a freshman at Georgetown Baptist College. After settling into dormitory life at Rucker Hall and becoming acquainted with the campus, I eagerly became active in the Maskrafter Drama Club. To my delight, I was selected to act in the play *The Book of Job.* Our intense rehearsals prepared us to perform not only at John L. Hill Chapel at Georgetown, but for several churches in Eastern Kentucky.

The *Western Recorder,* Kentucky's state Baptist paper, printed a feature article on our play, complete with a picture on the front cover of Bob Coleman, who played the part of Job. The article read in part:

> "The production is unique because of its all-scriptural lines, and the choral work of the players. No less unusual are the mosaic-like costumes and painted faces to look like stained-glass windows. The costuming is created for the production by Irene Corey, director of the college Art Department and wife of Professor Corey.
>
> This play will tour England and France July and August of 1958. Plans for the tour abroad are nearing completion. They call for a company of twelve selected from students and graduates.

I was shattered to learn I was not chosen to tour. It affected my total attitude toward college. I became discouraged and decided to leave. Besides, I wanted to become an airline stewardess, and a college education wasn't necessary for that. Before the semester was over, I hastily packed up and left.

Coming home was a letdown. All the kids I'd gone to school with were away, and there was nothing to do. Mother didn't mind my being home. We were in our own house now, and my room was waiting for me exactly as I'd left it. She and my stepfather Lee had carpeted and painted the little four-room house on the corner of Byers and Daviess.

After several interviews, I landed a job in the classified ads section of the *Messenger–Inquirer* newspaper. I began hearing rumors about a contest to select a queen for the Kentucky Derby. One day at work, Casper Gardner, vice-president of the Rotary Club, came to talk with me. He asked if his club could sponsor me in the contest. *Why not?* I thought, *it may take the edge off the boredom I am beginning to feel.*

To my utter delight and surprise I won the local contest. Now I would compete with fifteen other local winners in Louisville. My boss, Lawrence Hager, Sr., was most cooperative about my going. Mother drove me to Louisville, where I spent a whole week at the Watterson Hotel. Each day all the contestants were treated to luncheons, interviews, and photography sessions. Every outing was a time of being judged. After the first nervous jitters wore off, I decided there wasn't a chance for me to win this contest, so I began to relax and enjoy myself.

Soon the final evening of judging came. It was on a Saturday night in the General Electric Monogram Hall. Mother watched from the audience as each contestant was called on stage for a personal interview. Since my name was Travis and alphabetically last, I didn't get to see the other girls or hear their answers. When it was my turn, I adjusted the hoop beneath my borrowed white-net formal and concentrated on smiling and walking as gracefully as I could to the microphone.

Each judge asked a question. At first the questions were easy, but then one judge asked, "Miss Travis, can you tell me the name of the horse that won the Kentucky Derby in 1948?"

I paused and wondered how they expected me to have such information. Then I answered, "I'm sorry but I can't; I've never even been to a Derby." I sighed with relief when I heard the crowd laugh approvingly.

"Well, maybe you'll get to see one this year," the judge quipped.

The last judge stepped forward and quizzed me, "Tell me, Miss Owensboro, why would you want to be chosen as Miss Kentucky Derby Queen?"

I paused a moment to think through his provocative question. The answer clearly came to me, "I won't say that the lovely clothes, the $500 prize, and all the other things aren't attractive. Of course, you knew that, or they wouldn't have been offered. But I suppose the best reward would be to be able to represent Kentucky and be publicly proud of the state. I would hope Kentucky would be proud of me, too."

A spontaneous outburst of applause filled the auditorium as I made my exit smiling all the way. I assumed the audience had responded equally well to each girl. We were all standing behind the curtain waiting for the results. The suspenseful-sounding voice of the announcer called out the names of the five finalists, "Ann Shaver, Mary Kappas, Jeannetta MacDonald, Jan Buechler," and then I heard my name, "Pat Travis."

We were each presented a beautiful bouquet of long-stemmed red roses. My heart was pounding, and my mind raced with thoughts from the past week about each girl. Ann was so vivacious and had been unanimously chosen Miss Congeniality; Mary had thick, dark hair and a naturally tanned complexion; Jeannetta had angelic fine features; and Jan was always poised and self-assured. Standing among these girls was already an honor.

My smile began to tremble when I heard, "Ladies and Gen-

tlemen, Miss Kentucky Derby Queen of 1958 is . . ." You could
sense the anticipation, as he almost shouted, "Miss Owensboro,
Pat Travis!" Hot tears stung my eyes and spilled down my
cheeks. Finally, I floated across the stage through a sea of
camera flashes. Mother, her blue eyes sparkling, was waiting in
the wings.

The following morning the newspapers were filled with the
crowning and the events to follow. Miss Kentucky Derby
Queen would travel to Washington D.C. and New York City
to make personal appearances on the Ed Sullivan, Steve Allen,
and Dave Garroway shows. Of course, all this would follow a
shopping spree for a new wardrobe and the Coronation Ball in
Louisville.

Mother kept a scrapbook of pictures that was bulging by the
time I ended my reign. After reading some of the newsclippings,
I concluded that Dad's observation about exaggerated media
reports proved to be true. Some of my "so-called" quotes made
me laugh, such as the caption under one picture from New
York City. It went, "Pat Travis, Kentucky Derby Queen, finds
New York hectic and exhilarating." *My English teacher would
have dropped her teeth if I had ever used a vocabulary like that,*
I mused.

On March 25, 1958, I celebrated my nineteenth birthday in
Washington D.C., where I was representing Kentucky in the
Cherry Blossom Festival. While there I even had the honor of
going to the White House to present President Eisenhower an
official document adopting him into the Honorable Order of
Kentucky Colonels. However, Vice-President Richard Nixon
accepted it in his absence.

The final duty of my reign was to present roses to I. Valen-
zuela, the jockey who rode Tim Tam, winner of the 1958 Kentucky Derby. True to the judge's prediction, I did get to see my
first Kentucky Derby from the privileged vantage point of the
winner's circle on May 3 at the famous Churchill Downs in
Louisville.

Coming home to Owensboro and adjusting to normal life again was difficult. Soon, in my usual hasty manner, I made up my mind to fly to my father's home in California, where I could pursue an acting or modeling career. I should have taken more seriously the advice Dad had given me: "You're in trouble when you begin to believe your own publicity!"

Still, I felt a sense of obligation to the people in my hometown. I couldn't live up to their expectations in Owensboro. Maybe I could make it in California.

9

Romance in the Air

If you didn't know where 5731 Ranchito was, you'd miss it for sure. The only way to get to Dad and Bettie's new house was to drive down an almost-hidden driveway in Van Nuys. The sprawling ranch-style house was in what had once been an orange grove. Their property even included a two-bedroom guest house. They enjoyed the privacy of the secluded location.

The warm, braided rugs and rustic beamed ceilings provided a perfect setting for Dad's display of mounted moose, blesbok, caribou, and deer heads from hunting trips all over the United States and around the world.

Just looking at one massive moose head made me laugh. I'll never forget going to the airport with Dad to pick up his prize trophy. When we arrived in Dad's Cadillac convertible, there was no way to fit the giant crate in the trunk. So right in the airport, Dad had this brilliant idea of uncrating his beloved moose head, putting the top down, and placing it in the back seat.

Back in Kentucky, my uncles used to tie squirrel tails to the antennas of their cars to boast of their hunting skills. Today my Dad was driving through sunny Southern California, home of glamorous movie stars, with an Alaskan moose head in the back seat of his convertible. The moose's marble eyes stared back at the curious onlookers as Dad proudly drove home.

Bettie and her two sons, Dennis and Mike, met us in the driveway.

"Wow! He's a monster," Mike exclaimed.

"Just take a look at those antlers!" Dennis added.

Bettie laughed and teased, "I'm glad you didn't bring the rest of him home!"

There was only one problem. Dad's dear moose head was too big to fit through the door! Finally, we wrestled it through a double window we removed. Dear Mr. Moose found a resting place above the sofa where he became the obvious center of attention.

Dad had always enjoyed the outdoors and animals.

He even had a pet racoon called "Jigger" that lived in a cage in the backyard. Sometimes Jigger was allowed to come inside the house, but if he decided to roam independently it could be a chore to coax him back into captivity. Bettie became the favored animal trainer at this point. Jigger would oblige her command to crawl on her shoulder and be safely escorted back to his cage. Bettie's sons were always delighted by their mother's unscheduled performance and control of this wild animal. It was fun being included as part of this family with two young stepbrothers.

Dad was playing a show called "Town Hall Party," which was televised live every Saturday night from Compton, California. A roomy, barn-type building housed the show. It was complete with a huge dance floor that overflowed with fans.

When I went along, I usually stayed backstage talking to the performers. Joe and Rose Maphis were one of my favorite couples and close friends with Dad. (Joe recently died in Nashville and was buried there.) I loved to hear them sing, "What are little boys made of, my love?" Rosie would spontaneously throw in a line that would make Joe laugh, he'd act as if he were mad, and then think up something to get back at her. The audience enjoyed their antics.

The Collins Kids, Lawrencine and Larry, were a brother-and-sister act I adored. Their talent far exceeded their youth. Larry was so energetic that it wore me out watching as he'd point the neck of his guitar and bend his knees to dance rock-abilly-style across stage while playing like crazy! Lorrie, as we called her, had a gorgeous voice and was a perfectly poised young lady. She was surprisingly unspoiled in spite of the attention she constantly received from her fans.

Freddie Hart (best known for his later hit "Easy Lovin' ") was such a gentleman to talk to. He always dressed in a Western costume with a large heart on the front and back, outlined in sequins. His wavy black hair and dazzling smile made him a favorite with the ladies in the audience.

When Marilyn and Wesley Tuttle sang those good ol' gospel tunes, it reminded me of Pa Johnson's church back in Kentucky. They had a special glow about them, and they believed every word they were singing.

I enjoyed collecting black-and-white glossy fan pictures of all the Town Hall Party gang and having them personally autographed. Some even signed them to "Pat" instead of Patty, which I thought suited me better now that I was a "grownup" nineteen-year-old.

Bettie and I spent plenty of time together and often discussed my interest in modeling. She had recently completed a modeling course and found out about Adrian's, a popular teenage modeling agency in Pasadena. She made arrangements for me to go there and be interviewed.

Adrian was the stereotypical hard-nosed agent. He didn't seem impressed with my credentials as Kentucky Derby Queen, but he did offer me a job as a model and a secretary in his office. At least I would have a steady, if somewhat meager, income.

The long drive to Pasadena from Van Nuys was time consuming, and sharing Dad's car became a nuisance. After scouting the used car lots for days, I scraped enough money together for a down payment on a 1953 yellow Chevrolet convertible. The fact that it was five years old and it was nearly impossible to put the top up didn't bother me. I was in sunny California!

Soon I made the decision to move to Pasadena so I wouldn't have to fight the traffic every day. The only place I could afford to live on my salary was the YWCA. This particular "Y" served as a dormitory for many students from Pasadena City College. I asked for a private room, but the housemother informed me that that was unheard of. However, she promised I'd be alone until she had another request.

I'll never forget the first evening after I moved in. My boss, Mr. Adrian, invited me to a fancy Hollywood party. Making every effort to dress the part, I wore my orange wool knit dress with sling-back pumps and, of course, my mink stole that I'd won from the Derby Queen contest. I must have looked far out of character for the "Y." However, I wanted to impress my boss.

That evening when I came in, I flicked on the light to be startled by a pair of sleepy eyes staring quizzically up at me.

"Hi, I'm Lynne Nelson, your new roommate," the drowsy girl yawned apologetically. "The housemother said this was the only room left. I go to PCC. Would you please hurry and turn out the light? I've got an early class in the morning," added the blond stranger in big pink curlers.

Afterwards Lynne and I often laughed at our first unorthodox meeting. We had much in common and immediately became best friends. Even our dress and shoe sizes were the same, so we often traded clothing. By pooling our money, we managed to move out of the YWCA to an apartment.

I'd listen to Lynne's school and boyfriend problems, and she'd listen to my woes of trying to become "Millie the Model." My boss wasn't the easiest person in the world to get along with. He lost his temper at the least little things and threatened to fire me. Occasionally, I would leave the office and walk around the block while Mr. Adrian cooled off, but one day I walked out and didn't come back.

Lynne knew one of my desires was to become an airline stewardess (now called flight attendant). She read an ad that Trans World Airline was interviewing in Pasadena. With her encouragement, I made an appointment. When the airline called me for a second interview, I splurged on a brand-new seersucker suit with a white blouse, and even a hat to match. My hopes were high, and the disappointment of not being accepted was a horrible blow to my ego. They gave no explanation about why I was not chosen.

Next I found myself with an office job for the Avon Cosmetic Company in the traffic division. Not especially glamorous. However, something did come out of it. Brenda Engleman, a young married woman I worked with, was looking for a date for her husband's friend, Jack Gruben. She asked me to go out with him, and I accepted.

Jack was unpretentious and easy to be with. He was tall and lanky, and his strawberry blond hair was unruly. We found ourselves comfortable together, whether we were sharing a spaghetti supper with Dick and Brenda or waterskiing with a group of his friends.

One evening Jack and I double dated with his buddy from Tennessee. When Jack came to pick me up that evening, he was riding in his friend's white Lincoln convertible. Jack and I crawled in the backseat as he introduced me, "Pat, this is the guy I told you about from Tennessee, Gene Eatherly, and his girlfriend, Carolyn." I smiled. Jack continued his introduction, "Gene, you probably know Pat's father, being an ol' hillbilly from Nashville."

"Why sure, I used to work at the Grand Ole Opry," he answered. Jokingly nudging his girl friend, he remarked under his breath, "I sold peanuts and popcorn!" We all laughed.

Gene glanced around as the wind tossed my hair in every direction and asked, "Who's your dad?"

"Merle Travis," I answered.

"Merle who?"

"Merle Travis," I repeated. He wrote "Sixteen Tons." By now, I wished Jack had never breathed a word. It was embarrassing explaining to someone who was supposed to be impressed but obviously wasn't. I was ready to drop the subject.

"I think I've heard of him," Gene chuckled.

"Gene, not to change the subject, but do you suppose you could put your top up?" I asked. I had just done my hair and didn't like it blowing to bits. I don't think he liked my suggestion, but he stopped and put the top up on his car.

This would be my last evening out with Jack for awhile since he was leaving for six weeks at National Guard Camp. After he left, I was beginning to become lonesome until I had a call one evening from someone with a familiar-sounding voice.

"Hi Pat, remember me? Gene from Tennessee?"

I remembered.

"You know, I sure enjoyed meeting you. Sometimes I get homesick for a Southern accent. Jack tells me you're from Kentucky," he added.

"Yes, Owensboro, ever heard of it?" I teased.

"Sure, it's not far from my hometown, Nashville," Gene replied.

"Really? What are you doing in California?" I asked.

"Tell you what, how about us getting together for a drive Sunday afternoon? I'll tell you all about it," he suggested.

I thought about it for a moment and decided to accept. After all, Jack and I were only friends, and this guy seemed like he'd be fun to go out with.

"OK, it's a deal."

"Good, I'll pick you up at two o'clock. Bye."

"Bye, see you then," I confirmed and hung up. I felt a strange little flutter of excitement.

That Sunday afternoon I learned about Gene Eatherly. I liked what I saw. His strong, six-foot, two-inch build was obviously that of an athlete, and his dress showed pride and good taste. He was creative in his choice of where to take me. He'd chosen this lovely day to rent bicycles and ride around the Griffith Park Zoo. I had to struggle to keep up with him. Finally we stopped for a snow cone and found a quiet, tree-shaded spot to rest and talk.

"Gene, you promised to tell me how you happen to be living in California," I reminded him.

"Do you want the short version or the long version?" he laughed, looking into my eyes as if to analyze how interested I really was. Then he began. "We moved out here mainly because my stepfather is in the Merchant Marines and every-time he came into port, it was at the San Pedro Harbor in California. He got tired of making so many trips to Tennessee."

"What happened to your real father?" I questioned.

"He died when I was only six years old," Gene answered.

"So your mom and stepfather have been married most of your life?" I surmised.

"Yeah," he went on, "they married after my stepfather's wife died in childbirth. So I have a stepsister, Kathy. She's still in high school."

"Oh, do you have any more brothers or sisters?"

"Yes, Richard, is my older brother. He's married and lives back in Tennessee."

I could tell Gene was especially fond of his big brother.

"When did you move out to California?" I questioned.

"Well, let's see," Gene went on as he leaned against the shade tree. My folks moved out the year I graduated from high school in '54. I came out with them for the summer but went back to Middle Tennessee State College (now University) where I had a football scholarship. Ever heard of it?" he grinned.

I admitted I hadn't.

"It's in Murfreesboro, Tennessee . . . just thirty miles from Nashville. My grandmother lives in Nashville, and I knew I had a place to stay on holidays or weekends. But I hardly ever left school anyway."

Thoughtfully, I reflected on what he'd just said. "Aren't grandmothers special? I have a grandmother back in Kentucky who practically raised me."

"Yep, they are," he agreed, "I call mine 'Little Mama.' "

"Little Mama?" I chuckled. "How'd you come up with that?"

"Well, one of my grandmothers was big and fat; we called her 'Big Mama,' and the other one was little and skinny—and we called her 'Little Mama.' "

"Makes sense," I agreed. "Then what?" I prodded.

"After three years of football I started getting messed up with one injury after another. College football is tough, you know. I guess I got discouraged. One evening I called Mother in California and she suggested, 'Gene, you don't have to stay there and kill yourself; move out here with us, and you can finish your education here.'

"I went to Mount San Antonio Junior College in Walnut, California, for awhile. That's where I met Jack. But I lost so many credits when I transferred, it was hard to catch up. I dropped out and got a job." He added, "Maybe I'll still go back and get my degree some day." Then he reached over, squeezed my hand, and asked, "How about you?"

I told him about coming to California, hoping to make it in acting or modeling. "Now," I explained, "my main desire is to become an airline stewardess." There was much more I wanted to say, but it could wait. I had an intuitive feeling we were going to see plenty of each other.

10

Flying High

"I made it! I made it!" I shouted and sang and danced all over the apartment.

"Made what?" my roommate Lynne asked.

"United Airlines" was all I could answer. "I'm going to fly for United Airlines. I'm going to Cheyenne, Wyoming, for training to become an airline stewardess. Finally!"

"Congratulations!" Lynne exclaimed, "but what about you and Gene?"

Gene and I had become steady company, and it would be hard to leave him, but I had hoped for this opportunity.

"Things aren't all that serious," I shrugged. "Que sera, sera, whatever will be will be." Nothing was going to dampen my enthusiasm.

Soon I was enrolled in an intense training program. First I learned to tell time using the twenty-four-hour military method. For instance, one o'clock in the afternoon would be called 1300 hours. Then there were codes to learn representing every airport United flew into, such as LAX for Los Angeles. A mock cabin set up was used to teach serving skills, complete with teachers acting as irate passengers. One exciting aspect was learning to prepare for an emergency by evacuating through the windows and inflating a huge slide on the DC-8 jet. And of course, every potential trainee was taught the proper makeup, hair styles, and dress codes fitting for a United Airline stewardess.

On June 6, 1960, I was awarded my diploma and wings in a ceremony at the Brown Hotel in Denver, Colorado. My heart was set on moving to glamorous New York City or perhaps Chicago, but, unfortunately, the three girls I agreed to room with wanted to live in Los Angeles.

I thought it would be worth returning to California in order to share an apartment with these three girls. We were probably the only Southerners in stewardess training, and we were automatically drawn together. Joy Howell, from Waycross, Georgia, was tall, with naturally curly hair. She had a ready smile and a keen sense of humor flavored with genuine Southern charm. Donna Shea from Tulsa, Oklahoma, was the sophisticated one in the bunch. Then there was Jeane Sutter, our Houston, Texas, roommate with the kind, gentle personality.

Now came the difficult task of locating an apartment. If we each paid fifty dollars, we might be fortunate enough to find a two-bedroom apartment in Manhattan Beach, California. Everyone knew that's where all the pilots and "stews" lived. Fortunately, Joy owned a car. By this time I had sold mine to boost my finances.

Driving down the main drag in Manhattan Beach, we strained our eyes to spot "For Rent" signs.

"Hey, there's one," Jeane signaled.

Joy pulled to the curb, and we all piled out. Taking a deep, exaggerated breath, Donna said, "Just smell that fresh ocean air." We all nodded in agreement.

Finding our way to the apartment with the sign on the front door, I knocked.

"Yes, may I help you?" a deep voice asked as we looked into a suntanned face that would have put Robert Wagner to shame!

As we all stood there with our mouths gaping open, Joy decided to speak up. "We were just inquiring about y'all's apartment for rent," she drawled. "You see, we're going to be flying for United Airlines and wanted something close to the airport."

"Of course, come in, and I'll show you around. Actually this

place is split-level. There's a bedroom upstairs and downstairs.
You might enjoy the view from up here," he said, pointing to
the picture window framing the Pacific Ocean in the distance.
You could even see people playing volleyball on the beach.
"There's a nice, cozy fireplace here in the corner for those cool
California evenings."

Gathering courage to talk about practical matters, I asked,
"How much is the rent?"

"The rent?" he asked. "Oh, yes, it's four hundred dollars a
month, plus utilities."

We gulped in unison. That was twice the amount we could
afford. "I'm afraid that's a bit steep for our salaries," I admitted, "but it sure is a nice place."

As he walked us to the door, the handsome man explained,
"Quite honestly, this is not my place. I'm showing it for the
owner. My roommate moved recently, and if I could find another guy to share the rent, I could stay downstairs, and he could
have the upstairs. If you know of anybody, tell them to give me
a call." He quickly wrote his phone number down and handed
it to me.

When we got in the car, Joy teasingly said, "Well, at least
we've got his number! I think I'm going to like Manhattan
Beach. How 'bout a bite to eat, y'all? I'm starved."

We drove back into Inglewood near the airport and stopped
at a coffee shop for lunch. Settling into a booth near the back
of the restaurant, we were all looking over the menus trying to
make up our minds, when a familar voice called my name. I
looked up to see a welcome smile from Gene Eatherly. "Gene!"
I nearly shouted. "What on earth are you doing here?"

"I was about to ask you the same question," he answered.
"Are you a stewardess now?"

"I sure am, just wait till you see me in my snazzy blue
uniform," I boasted proudly. "And these are my new roommates, Donna Shea, Joy Howell, and Jeane Sutter."

Gene joined us for lunch, and we learned that he had just

been promoted with U.S. Rubber Company and had been transferred to this area. By coincidence he too was looking for an apartment. We told him about the place on the beach that we couldn't afford.

"Don't worry, there's plenty of places around here. You'll find something good," he added.

That was encouraging to hear. It was good to see Gene again and know that he would be around. I had to admit I'd kind of missed him. Before we left, I gave him the number where we were staying temporarily.

"Now back to the drawing board," Joy coaxed. "Come on, we're going to Manhattan Beach and find an apartment we can afford."

And we did, only two doors from the expensive one. How was I to know Gene would rent the super deluxe model so close by?

11

Clipped Wings

Months had passed . . . and now I was parading down the aisle of United Airlines' DC-8 Jet Mainliner. It was a special joy today, because I was wearing my brand-new engagement ring. I intentionally used my left hand to collect compliments about the diamond Gene had given me for my twenty-second birthday. He had teasingly remarked he couldn't think of anything else to give me! I was happy he had surprised me instead of asking me first. He'd made my decision for me. But now many of my friends and passengers were asking me when we planned to be married. Married? We were so excited about our engagement we really hadn't discussed our wedding plans. *When I get home from this flight, I'm going to pin him down to a date,* I thought.

The only negative aspect about marriage was it would end my airline career. (Of course, that policy was later changed, and many married women are flight attendants today.) Everyone knew the rule that only single girls could fly. When you married, your "wings were clipped." United even had a club for former stewardesses called "Clipped Wings."

Oh, well, many more flights like this one, and I will be glad to be confined to earth. This trip is a killer. We left Los Angeles at midnight to fly to Las Vegas, where we picked up a rowdy group en route to Chicago. Before landing in Chicago, we served breakfast to those we could awaken. Inevitably, the same passengers, who waved us off by claiming not to be hungry for breakfast, smelled bacon and eggs and decided to have a tray after all. Of course, this completely messed up the routine of our service. Somehow, we'd manage to accomplish this portion of our schedule, then wait two hours at O'Hare Airport in Chicago to fly the last leg of our journey to Baltimore, Maryland, with a fresh load of passengers. When we finally arrived exhausted, we were shuttled to a nearby hotel to sleep the required layover before flying back to California. After ten months of this work, I sometimes questioned my sanity in thinking this was a "glamorous" job.

This time I was eager to get back to Los Angeles, especially since Gene would be picking me up at the airport. We had much to talk about. As soon as I walked through the stewardess' lounge, there he was. "How was your flight?" he asked as we walked to his car.

"Oh, fine," I lied. "But I can't wait to kick off my shoes and relax. It seems like I've been gone a month. Guess what I learned from the stew I flew with this trip?"

"What?" he inquired, putting his arm around me as we drove out of the parking lot toward Manhattan Beach.

"She said that after we are married, we will be entitled to a trip pass anywhere United flies, except Hawaii. She called it a honeymoon pass. How does that sound?"

"Great," he responded. "Where should we go?"

"Let's go as far as United flies. How about Miami, Florida?"

"How about going to Nassau from there," he added. "It couldn't cost much from Florida. Maybe you could get us discount tickets."

By the time we arrived at my apartment, we were making honeymoon plans before we had even made wedding plans! I invited Gene in to continue our conversation.

"You know, Gene, we need to set a wedding date." I went on, "It's embarrassing when people compliment my ring and then ask, 'When's the date?' What am I supposed to tell them? To tell you the truth, I don't care if it's next year, next month, or tomorrow. I just want to know when."

I couldn't believe I'd been so forward, but I had expressed my deep-down feelings. Now I was waiting for his response.

"Where's a calendar?" he asked.

"A what?"

"A calendar," Gene repeated. "I need to figure my next vacation. I found one in the kitchen and we sat down together to look at it.

"Let's see, I've got two weeks coming the first part of August," he mused, studying the dates. Then he looked up at me and asked, "How does August 4 sound? That's a Friday and a weekend."

"August 4, 1961. Why not? Sounds good to me. We've got a lot of planning to do. Maybe we should keep it simple and just go to a justice of the peace or have one of those backyard weddings," I suggested.

"No, I don't think so," Gene reasoned. "You only get married once; I think it should be in church."

"Church? What church? I haven't been to church since I moved out here," I admitted.

"We'll find a place. Maybe one of those pretty little glass chapels that you see around . . . you know, like the one Jayne Mansfield and Mickey Hargitay recently got married in out at Pacific Palisades."

That started our search for the perfect little glass chapel we could afford. My budget also started as I made a long list of expenses. There would be the cake, the flowers, the invitations, my dress, and the list grew and grew. I planned to save enough money each payday to handle these items one at a time.

Now to call and tell Mom. She'd heard all about Gene in my letters and had even met him when she flew out for a brief visit a couple of months earlier. She wasn't really surprised, but was eager to help all she could.

"Patty," she said, "remember that white embroidered organdy dress you wore when you were Kentucky Derby Queen?"

I remembered.

"I've kept it safe in the attic, and it would make a beautiful bridal gown. Let me send it to you, and you can take it to the dry cleaner. That would save you loads of money."

When the gown came in the mail, I rushed it to the cleaner, where I always took my airline uniforms. The lady who worked there knew me as a frequent customer. We talked about my plans for this dress, and she assured me that it would come out like new. Her daughter had recently married, and the nice lady offered to loan me her daughter's bridal veil and petticoat. Now, all I needed was new white shoes.

Little by little, I paid faithfully on each item for the wedding. Gene and I even found La Tijera Methodist Church in Inglewood, which was the perfect glass and rock chapel. The church had a well-appointed adjoining room for receptions. For a small additional fee, the church would provide the punch and decorations. The minister, William J. Delaney, set a time for a premarital counseling session with us before the wedding.

Dr. Delaney folded his hands and looked at us across his desk. He held a white booklet called *In Holy Matrimony.* "I want to give you this booklet," he began, "but before I do, let me tell you how glad I am that you have chosen to come to a Christian minister to be married. You might have gone to a justice of the peace or another civil officer. You didn't, and that shows you recognize the importance of religion in marriage."

I avoided looking at Gene. I wondered if the preacher could read the guilt on my face after his statement.

Dr. Delaney continued, "Pat, will your father be giving you away?"

"Oh, yes, sir," I answered. He plans to walk me down the aisle, and our good friend, Wesley Tuttle, will sing. My roommates, Donna Shea and Jeane Sutter, will be my bridesmaids and Joy Howell, my maid of honor. We've been working on the plans."

"How about you, Gene, who will be your best man?" asked Dr. Delaney.

"My brother, Richard, is coming in from Nashville," Gene replied, "and my other attendants are Wayne Natale and Randy Harris. Ron Sage and Pat's stepbrother, Dennis Robinson, will be ushers."

Dr. Delaney wrote their names down and scheduled a rehearsal date. He stood and shook hands with Gene, gave me the booklet, and told us to call if we had any questions.

As we left, we admired the beautiful little chapel. We began discussing how things should be after we married. We even talked about our views of raising children. That's when we came to the conclusion that, if or when we ever had children, we would take them to church. Our mothers had taken us, and we felt it was good for kids.

12

All Worked Up

The early-morning August air blew through the windows of Gene's new black 1961 Ford Falcon. He had sacrificially traded his white Lincoln convertible to be more practical now that we were married. "Can't afford you and the Lincoln, too," he teased.

I laid my head on Gene's shoulder as we sped south on Kentucky Highway 431 heading toward Nashville. After a romantic week in Nassau, Bahamas, we chose to spend our second week getting acquainted with each others' relatives in Kentucky and Tennessee. We'd been treated royally with food fit for a king at Mom and Lee's. Every meal was a feast of fresh corn, homegrown tomatoes, green beans, fried chicken, or country ham, topped off with Mom's banana pudding.

"A penny for your thoughts, Mrs. Eatherly," Gene whispered softly in my ear.

"They're worth more than that," I smiled. "How'd you like meeting all my kinfolks?" I asked.

"Well, let's see; there's your Uncle Kenneth, the truck driver, and your Uncle Lelan Ray, the coal miner, then the preacher uncle; what's his name?"

"Elgie," I reminded him. My mother named him when he was born. His full name is Elgie Lucilas Johnson."

Gene chuckled, "Now that's a country-sounding name if I've ever heard one."

"That's nothing compared with my great grandmother; her name is Queen Idella Sofronia Lonnie Sumner! As a matter of fact, she doesn't live too far from here," I commented, sitting

79

up and observing the road we were on more closely. We'd just driven through Drakesboro, a tiny coal-mining community. "If it isn't too early, maybe we could stop and visit her," I suggested. "She and my Great Aunt Evalee live together near here."

"Please, spare me," Gene pleaded, "no more relatives for awhile."

All of a sudden, Gene stiffened his posture and put both hands on the steering wheel. Glancing in the rearview mirror, he asked, "Do you see what I see? Someone is following us. Just when we passed by that small group of houses back down the road, I noticed an old man get out of his porch swing and into his car. He's chasing us," Gene said as he slowed down.

When I turned around to look, the old man placed a red flashing light on the dashboard of his fifteen-year-old Chevrolet and signaled us to pull over.

"Oh, no," I groaned. "I bet we were speeding."

Gene stopped on the side of the road as the old man pulled up behind us. We watched him open his car door, step out as he spit chewing tobacco on the ground, and mosey over to the driver's window. "Whar y'all a'goin' in such a hurry?"

Before Gene could get a word out, the old man continued, "You didn't even slow down fer that blinkin' yeller light back yonder."

"What blinking yellow light?" Gene asked, not meaning to sound disrespectful.

"Why, the only one in town; and you went right through it! Whar 'bouts y'all headed?"

"We're headed to Nashville, Sir, to visit my brother." Gene answered diplomatically.

"I see by your license plate that your're from California," he added suspiciously.

I leaned over and explained, "We just married in California, but I'm from Owensboro."

"Well, you're trav'lin' way too fast fer these here parts. I'm goin' hafta take y'all to see the judge," he ordered.

"The judge?" Gene asked, surprised.

"Yep. Jest follow me."

Gene cautiously followed as I alertly examined where we were. "Why, he's taking us back into Drakesboro. This is where I was telling you that my Aunt Evalee and my great grandmother live. I bet he knows them. Maybe we can talk him out of a ticket," I schemed.

Gene looked at his watch. "It's not even six o'clock yet. Looks like the whole town's asleep." Looking around, Gene said, "Surely he's not taking us to the judge's house. If so, maybe the judge will be asleep, too," he added wishfully.

We turned down an unpaved street and stopped in front of an aged, soot-stained frame house, shadowed by giant shade trees. We gently closed the car doors, so we wouldn't disturb the judge. Walking a few paces behind the old man on the path to the house, I initiated a conversation.

"You know, Sir," I began, "all my people are from around here." Trying to impress him, I volunteered, "I bet you know my father, Merle Travis."

He stopped and turned around, and I studied his expression. It didn't change.

I continued, "They had a homecoming for him not too long ago down in Ebenezer."

Still no change of expression. All he did was sort of grunt.

I carried on, "You might know my Aunt Evalee Shutt; she cooks at the schoolhouse in Drakesboro."

Finally he responded, "Whose girl are you?"

"My mother was Mary Johnson," I offered.

Thoughtfully, he pushed his hands deep into his pockets, kind of frowned, as if remembering, and asked, "Johnson? Wuz she any kin to Preacher Will?"

"Yes, sir," I quickly answered, more encouraged. "He's my Grandpa."

His whole face lit up. "You mean you're Preacher Will's gran'daughter?"

"Yes sir," I smiled proudly.

"Well, I'll be! Imagine that!" He shook his head unbelieving, then repeated, "Preacher Will's gran'daughter."

I caught a glimpse of Gene's puzzled look. I could tell he was amused that Merle Travis hadn't impressed him, but Preacher Will had.

Gene now entered into the discussion, "It's awfully early, Sir. The judge is probably still asleep. I'd hate for you to wake him up."

The old man rammed his hands a little deeper into his pockets and nervously kicked a rock by his foot. "Did ya say y'all jest got married?"

"Yes, we did," Gene answered.

Reluctant to make eye contact, the man mumbled, "Why, I reckon you're still on your honeymoon."

"Well, yes, we are," Gene confirmed his statement.

Then the man looked down to kick the rock again, glanced toward the obvious unwakened house, took a deep breath, and with hesitation in his voice, thought out loud, "I reckon I ort to let y'all go this time."

Gene and I stood there partially relieved, waiting to hear the final verdict.

Sounding slightly embarrassed, the old man concluded, "Shucks, if you're still on your honeymoon, I reckon you're jest all worked up!"

13

Suddenly Strangers

Cooking supper for my new husband was quite a challenge, especially since I didn't own a stove! But I didn't mind. Among our wedding gifts were a portable oven and an electric skillet. What else did I need? Those suited our casual needs and my cooking skills adequately.

Gene and I enjoyed the guest house Dad generously allowed us to move into behind his home. We'd painted and hung curtains until it looked like an oversized doll house. Once during the "fixing-up" stage, Grandpa and Ramona Jones and their son Mark were visiting Dad and Bettie. Five-year-old curious Mark wandered back to see what we were doing. Gene was balanced on a ladder painting the exposed beam ceiling. After a long period of quiet observation, young pint-sized Mark squinted up through his thick glasses and, in his nasal little voice, offered, "Patty, is thar anythang I kin do to hep ya?" Being a wife was fun!

However, late one evening, only a few months after moving in, something happened that cut an indelible scar into my memory. Gene and I were cuddled up on the sofa after supper watching television like a couple of lovebirds. Since there was no air conditioning, the door was open to allow the cool breezes in. Suddenly the screen door flew open, and we were startled to see Dad stagger in. We'd become acutely aware of and sometimes involved in problems that surfaced due to his excessive drinking. Tonight his speech was blurred, and his eyes were glassy. He wanted our full attention and demanded we turn off the television.

Gene quietly tried to persuade him to leave when Dad lashed out incoherently, "Who da ya think ya are tryin' to tell me wha' I can do?" His speech was thick and alarming as he waved his bottle of beer in the air.

He was weaving so badly I was afraid he might fall. Pretending to be calm, I jumped up and steadied my father. I insisted, "Let us help you back to your house." Gene reacted immediately to my desperate look for assistance.

Together we determinedly guided him through our door into the dark. The back porch light of the main house cast a dim glow on Dad's distorted face. He seemed agreeable for a moment, then jerked loose and smashed his unfinished beer bottle against the sharp edge of the house.

We both dodged the flying, broken glass and stared in disbelief. He began making serious threats. "Dad!" I heard my voice rise and tremble. "Do you know who you're talking to? I'm your daughter!"

My rationale didn't faze him. The curve of his lips snarled like a trapped animal, and he slurred, "I could kill ya and I would kill ya, and don'cha ferget it!"

Suddenly my own father seemed like a stranger. Fear stung my heart, and my knees went limp. With an unexpected surge of strength, Dad pushed open his back door and rushed in.

Terrified I turned to Gene, "Do you suppose he's going to get a gun?"

"We're not waiting to find out; we're getting out of here!"

Gene ran into our house, grabbed the car keys, we raced barefoot to our car, and sped out the driveway. The logical place to go for help was the police station. But after reporting our experience we were told there was nothing they could do. They explained to us that "the man," as they called Dad, was on his own property and had not broken any laws.

Stunned by this information, we then drove to counsel with Dad's doctor, Dr. Wendell Starr, who was also a family friend and had attended our wedding only a short time before. Dr.

Starr sympathetically listened, then advised us not to go back right away. "In Merle's intoxicated state," the doctor stated, "he doesn't realize anything he is saying or doing." Then as kindly, but as straightforwardly as possible, he added, "In his condition, he could harm the ones he loves most."

We climbed back into our car and drove around, not knowing where to go or what to do. Since Gene's mother lived only an hour away, we decided to go there to spend the night.

After a sleepless night, we concluded that we would have to move from the guest house into an apartment. We returned the next afternoon to pack our belongings, only to find Dad hurt and insulted. He seemed oblivious to the past evening's events. Our reasoning seemed irrational to him, and he accused us of deserting a sick man.

The sickness of alcohol had overcome Dad. As much as Gene and I wished we could help him, we had to be concerned for our own safety.

Fortunately, it didn't take long to find a new apartment. It was small, but comfortable, and only seventy-five dollars a month. There were three other young couples in the complex, and we made close friends with them. Since there was little left in our budget for entertainment, we enjoyed getting with our new friends for a game of Tripoley on Saturday nights.

Like many young couples we were constantly trying to find ways of saving money. Our goal was to save enough for a down payment on our own home. I accepted a job as a receptionist for Key Personnel Employment Agency. During my interview, I assured my boss, Helen Guerin, that my husband and I didn't plan on starting a family for years. That certainly made it difficult to break the news to her only months later of my unscheduled pregnancy.

Gene and I were delighted to be prospective parents. It was the topic of our conversation over the candlelight dinner I'd prepared of sauerkraut and wieners on our first anniversary. My waistline was barely hinting at being tight. I could hardly wait to wear those cute maternity clothes I'd already been admiring.

That time came sooner than I'd imagined, and during my eighth month Gene came home with news which caused a mixture of feelings. "Honey," he announced proudly, "your husband has been promoted!"

I threw my arms around him—or tried to—since something (Or should I say, someone?) had come between us. My tummy was so big now, even a hug required special skill. "I'm proud of you, Gene. Tell me more about it," I inquired.

He held my hand and seated me on the sofa beside him. Then he began explaining that he would be selling tires to copper mining companies.

"Copper mines?" I questioned. "Where are there any copper mines?"

"Well, that's the only problem," he explained sheepishly. "They're in my new territory in Southern Arizona." Before I could collect my thoughts and respond intelligently, he added, "We'll be moving to Tucson."

"Tucson, Arizona? But I'm eight months pregnant; what about my doctor? And it's almost Christmas . . . and isn't that the desert? I've never even been to Tucson in my life!"

"Don't worry, Honey, they have doctors there, too. This is my big chance to make some good money. I bet you'll like the desert. Besides," he went on encouraging me, "we have nearly $1,000 in the bank. When we get to Tucson, we could buy our own home before the baby comes." Now that did appeal to me.

He continued, "I've heard real estate is cheaper there than it is here in the San Fernando Valley."

We made the move as uncomplicated as possible. I didn't bother to tell Dad. Gene was right. As soon as we moved, we scouted the residential area from our temporary quarters of the Tideland Motor Inn.

When Mother and Lee found out that Gene and I were spending Christmas alone in a strange city motel, they drove

2,000 miles from Kentucky to join us so we wouldn't be lonesome. It was like Santa's sleigh arriving in the desert when Mother and Lee showed up. They not only unloaded and decorated an artificial tree for our adjoining motel rooms but also completed it with gifts. Most of the gifts consisted of necessities for their expected grandbaby. Gene plunged into the spirit and purchased a wreath for the door. To our utter dismay, someone stole it! I knew I would never forget those unusual holidays.

Lee's experience as a carpenter in the building business helped guide our choice for the best house and the best price. Soon we had signed a contract to become homeowners. Although our meager savings didn't completely meet the requirements, the seller allowed us to take a second mortgage. I saved the multiple listing write-up which read:

Please inspect this one. It will sell if shown. Has beautiful formal patio fully landscaped, complete with fish pond. Separated drying yard and play area. Palm trees and roses in front yard plus shade trees front and rear. Former owner spent $4,000 in improvements, plus his labor.

We were proud of our spacious three-bedroom residence at 432 South Alandale in a suburb called Sherwood Village. Although the original asking price was $15,000, we felt we'd found a bargain when our $13,000 offer was accepted.

Only a week or so after Mother and Lee left, the moving van arrived, and Gene and I settled into our new home. On February 9, 1963, Dawn Elizabeth Eatherly was born. Mother flew back to Tucson to help care for me and her first granddaughter. My independent spirit grew weary of Mom's advice, and I longed to be alone with my baby.

When she left, however, my mother-in-law came to take charge. She arrived with more baby-care instructions, complete with an outdated supply of bellybands to assure a flat navel.

My mother-in-law encouraged me to breast feed instead of

bottle feed. "Now, Pat, Honey," she began listing the advantages, "nursing is much healthier for the baby." She continued with her speech of how the infant receives natural immunities from the mother's body, and then somewhere in her lecture, I heard, ". . . and it also helps the uterus to go back in place sooner, causing your stomach muscles to flatten your tummy."

That did it. "OK," I obediently obliged, "if you think it's such a good idea, I'll try it." I've never regretted that decision.

Soon, my wish became a reality and I was alone with my baby girl. Then I realized how much both mothers had helped. How could one tiny infant create so much work?

Only fifteen months later, May 27, 1964, another daughter was born. We named her Paige Lorraine Eatherly. My mother was having health problems and wasn't able to come. Gene's mother couldn't come this time, either. I was on my own. I began to learn a very practical lesson on "Mother Appreciation."

14

Everything for a Purpose

The summer of '65 we packed diaper bags, babies, and suit-
cases, and made the long journey to Kentucky and Tennessee.
It was an economical vacation, and we enjoyed visiting our
families and catching up on all the news. Gene's brother, Richard, was doing especially well financially. He, his wife Faye, and
their five children were living in a beautiful two-story home.
Richard was excited about the money he was making selling
stock to capitalize a new insurance company. Gene and I were
impressed to see him wearing tailor-made suits and driving a
new El Dorado. Richard tried to convince Gene to move back
to Nashville and work with him. The idea was planted in my
husband's mind.

On our long trip home to Tucson, we reminisced about our
visit. "Do you really think we'd ever move back like Richard
was talking about?" I asked.

"Who knows? Maybe if the price is right," Gene answered.
"There's no reason I couldn't do as well as my brother. He's
never even been in sales before."

Thoughtfully, I projected that such a move would put the
girls closer to their "Mam-ma," as Mother had lovingly taught
our daughters to call her. "She and Lee would spoil them
rotten," I laughed.

Remembering our stay in Owensboro, I asked, "Wasn't that
sweet of Lee to build a miniature table and chairs for Dawn and
Paige?"

"Lee enjoys doing that sort of thing," Gene responded. "I
still can't believe you have so many relatives," he exclaimed. "I

think your mother invited the whole state of Kentucky to see the kids."

"I know," I smiled.

Gene tended to the tiresome task of driving while I handled the chore of child care. Finally, we were back home in Tucson. My salesman husband was soon back on the road, making his calls in the now familiar desert territory, and I settled into my routine homemaker role.

Our once-spacious home seemed to shrink with two children. My life became filled with mountains of toys to trip over, meals of strained baby food, and sunny afternoon strolls. Since Dawn was the older, I taught her to stand on the back of the stroller to free the seat for her baby sister, Paige. It was almost like having twins.

There was one major habit change since our children were born. That was church attendance. We were true to our promise to each other about taking kids to church. It was fun to dress Dawn and Paige alike in ruffles and frills and see them toddle off to Sunday School. I knew this pleased Mother, because she'd stressed to me again how important this training was in a child's life.

We didn't know the people at our church very well, but we did become well acquainted with our neighbors. Ours was a young neighborhood with many children. We'd often trade baby-sitting and entertain with a cookout in someone's backyard. Even with Gene gone so often, I was never lonesome for friends.

However, it was always a welcome sight to see my husband drive into the carport on Fridays after his week on the road. One such evening he was the bearer of rather disappointing news. He had stopped in for a drink at a local Safford, Arizona, night club that he occasionally visited on his trips. That particular night, Merle Travis was performing. I listened as Gene told me about their brief conversation. All Gene reported was that Dad asked how I was, then inquired about the children. His

Merle Robert Travis and Mary Elizabeth Johnson—married on April 12, 1937 (Mary was seventeen. Merle, nineteen).

Patricia Adeline Travis, born March 25, 1939—notice the Travis ears!

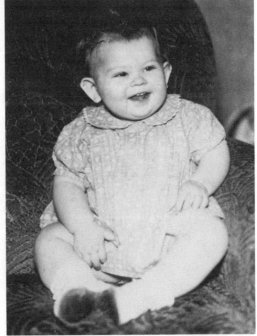

Bivie Adeline Johnson and "Preacher" Will Johnson, Pat's maternal grandparents.

A rare family portrait of Patty with her parents, Merle and Mary Travis—taken in Cincinnati, Ohio (1942).

Patty with her mother, Mary—a jealous stepfather cut Merle out of the left side of the picture.

"The Drifting Pioneers" on WLW Radio (Cincinnati) in the early 1940s—(left to right) Merle Travis, Bill Brown, Sleepy Marlin, and Walt Brown.

MERLE TRAVIS HOMECOMING CELEBRATION—1946—Patty holds the key to the city of Drakesboro, Kentucky, which her daddy was rewarded for his hit song, "Smoke, Smoke, Smoke (That Cigarette)." Bunnie Baugh wears Merle's hat while Mose Rager and Tex Atchinson look on.

"Cowgirl" Patty shares a stump with her best friend, Reda Ann Brown, South Hill, Kentucky (1948).

Patty's first TV appearance on the "Merle Travis & Company Show"—standing between her father and stepmother, June (1953).

Proud Patty with her two little half-sisters, Merlene and Cindy. Merlene—born October 8, 1949 Cindy—born April 26, 1952.

Pat's mother, Mary, and stepfather, George Lee Edwards—they were wed on December 31, 1955.

June 29, 1956, at Ebenezer, Kentucky—MERLE TRAVIS DAY—Patty unveils a monument honoring her father's song, "Sixteen Tons."

Gene Autry visits with Pat at the Merle Travis Day celebration, Ebenezer, Kentucky.

Merle and his wife, Bettie Lou, at the Merle Travis Day in Ebenezer. Her sons, Dennis and Mike Robinson, feel the impact of flashbulbs.

Merle constantly drew cartoons. Here he illustrated five of his songs, Sixteen Tons; So Round, So Firm, So Fully Packed; Smoke, Smoke, Smoke (That Cigarette); Kentucky Means Paradise; and Divorce Me C.O.D. (Used courtesy of American Music, Inc.)

Kentucky Derby Queen Pat Travis celebrated with Kentucky's Governor A. B. (Happy) Chandler and entertainer Art Linkletter.

1958 Kentucky Derby Queen and Court—left to right—Pat Travis, Ann Shaver, Mary Kappas, Jeannetta McDonald, and Jan Buechler.

Vice-president Richard Nixon smiled as he was commissioned a Kentucky Colonel at his office in Washington, D.C. With Nixon and Pat was Kentucky Republican representative, John M. Robinson.

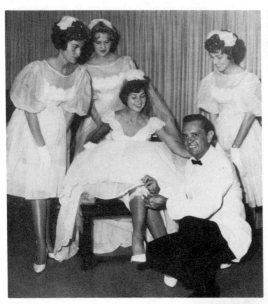

Merle adjusts Pat's garter before the wedding. (August 4, 1961). Looking on are Joy Howell, Donna Shea, and Jeane Sutter.

The happy bride and groom, Mr. and Mrs. Gene Eatherly.

Tricia with Grandfather Merle at the Johnnie High Show in the Will Rogers Memorial Center, Fort Worth, Texas.

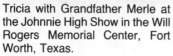

Pat enjoys a recent visit with Chet Atkins, a longtime friend of her father's.

A special letter, complete with caricature Merle drew especially for his granddaughter, Tricia Eatherly.

Merle and Pat holding the key to Merle Travis Day in Drakesboro, Kentucky.

The Eatherly family portrait in 1982—Gene and Pat in front and (left to right, standing) Paige, Dawn, and Tricia.

very words were, "Now, what is it y'all have? Was it two girls or two boys?"

After I heard that, I didn't want to hear any more. When Dawn was only four months old we'd made a special effort to visit Dad. We openly showed our love and affection. Dad seemed responsive at the moment. "She's a pretty little thing— just like her mam-ma," he'd boasted. However, he'd made no attempt on his own to keep in touch with us. Why couldn't he have cared enough to drive the short distance from Safford to Tucson? I laughed to cover the hurt. I was growing used to pretending Dad's disinterest didn't matter.

Days went by, then turned into weeks, and weeks into months until Christmas was once again around the corner. I knew I would be hearing from Mother asking for gift suggestions for the girls.

I did hear from her, but it wasn't as I'd expected. I had just walked home from visiting a friend down the street. As I was turning the key to unlock the door I heard the phone ringing. I hurried in and picked up the receiver, "Hello."

"Hi, Sug," his way of saying sugar. It was Lee. It was good to hear his voice. "How are y'all doing?" he asked.

"Oh, all right. Is everything OK back there?" I questioned. Mother usually called.

"Well, not really." He sounded a little shaky. I began to feel uneasy.

"Now, Patty (he and Mom refused to call me Pat), your Mother doesn't want you to worry, but remember when we told you about her hysterectomy?"

"Yes." I remembered. It had been the first part of November. I thought she was doing well.

Lee went on, "She had to be put back in the hospital for another operation. She had surgery to remove a growth."

"A growth? What kind? Where? Will she be all right?"

"She's going to be all right," he answered before I could voice my questions. "But the doctors said it is malignant."

Malignant? That meant cancer, I reasoned.

"Now, Patty," Lee continued before I could speak, "they removed all they could, and they will be giving her cobalt treatments to take care of the rest. She doesn't want you to worry."

"Lee, I wish I could be there." He now seemed so far away. "Tell Mom I'll call her right away."

"Okay, Sug, I'll let you go now. Bye."

"Bye," I said, dreading to hang up.

Why was Gene always out of town when I needed him? I checked the calendar. He would be driving in from Bisbee tonight. Sometimes I felt angry toward his work schedule of being gone every other week. I needed him *now.*

By the time Gene drove in, I had calmed down a bit. We talked about the possibility of my going to Owensboro. It seemed overwhelming to make arrangements for the children, plus the exorbitant expense of flying.

"Honey, didn't Lee say your mother is getting good treatment in the hospital?" Gene implored.

"Yes," I nodded.

"Well, why don't we just wait and see? She might need you more later." That sounded logical.

"Besides," Gene reminded me, "we'll be going back again this summer, six months from now."

I felt better. I would wait.

The first letter I received from Mother after her operation was full of cheerful news of friends, family, and flowers. Her main concern seemed to be arranging for someone to shop for her granddaughters' Christmas presents.

Parts of her letter read like this:

> "Sug, my stay in the hospital sure was nice. Everybody was so good, and they did everything possible to make me comfortable. I only wish you could have been here to visit me. I am an outpatient now. I will have a cobalt treatment

every day for six weeks. This growth was so large they couldn't remove it all. But God has blessed me so far, and I'm not in too much pain. They hope to clear this up within six weeks, but it all depends on how I can take it. I think everything is for a purpose. Sometimes we wander too far from God. I hope always to be near, not just when I'm sick, but at all times.

She concluded with,

You and Gene pray and live close to God each day of your life so you will be richly blessed, for things we want are so little compared to what God has to offer us.

Only a loving Father in heaven could have known how desperately I needed to be moved from Arizona to my mother's side in Kentucky. The idea seemed out of the question. Gene had just begun establishing his reputation as a top salesman with U.S. Rubber Company. His Southern Arizona territory was proving to be profitable with its tire sales to the copper mines. Gene had met and even doubled his sales quota for last year. But the company raised his quota the following year to a seemingly unreachable amount.

Richard began to call more frequently about Gene's working with him in the insurance business in Nashville. The offer began to sound lucrative, and the timing seemed right for this challenge. Gene was convinced it would be an opportunity of a lifetime to start on the ground floor with World Heritage Life Insurance Company.

By March 1966 we'd sold our Tucson home, packed a U-Haul, and headed for a straight-commission job in Nashville, Tennessee.

For Gene, it was like going back home. For me, it would mean being near Mother.

15

Stepfather—Real Father

After we settled into our modest rented duplex in Nashville, I drove the 150 miles to Owensboro with Dawn and Paige to visit Mother and Lee. It was going to be so convenient to be only three hours away. Mother's blue eyes sparkled with happiness in her new grandmother's role. But on the second day of our visit something terrible happened. With no apparent warning, her excruciating pain forced us to rush Mother back to the hospital. After some uncomfortable examinations, adhesions were discovered to be obstructing her colon. Fourteen inches of her small intestine had to be removed.

When the tedious surgery was finally over I watched helplessly as Mother was wheeled from recovery into a hospital room. There was a gavage tube in her nose for suction of gastric juices and the usual intravenous setup attached to her arm. It was all foreign and frightening to me. I sought comfort in the professional skills being administered by the hospital staff. However, that comfort soon crumbled when Mother's stitches pulled open. She was rushed back to surgery to be repaired with clamps. This technique also failed. What had gone wrong?

I recalled that Mother's first operation had been in November 1965 when she'd had a hysterectomy. Afterwards, hormones had been prescribed, and she had taken them faithfully. When symptoms of bowel problems had surfaced, she had gone back to the doctor. A simple rectal examination detected a massive growth. The fact that it had grown so rapidly was explained as due to the large dosage of hormones. Surgery had been performed to remove this growth in December 1965. Tests revealed it was malignant. Since it was impossible to remove the growth completely, cobalt treatments had been given to prevent the cancer from spreading. Mother had taken a treatment every day for six weeks, except on weekends. Her doctors had even voiced an assurance of this treatment as a cure.

All indications of her tolerance to the treatments had pointed to the hope of regained health, and her vital signs had appeared favorable. At least until now.

I felt forlorn and frustrated. It was difficult to interpret the medical jargon when I asked questions. Finally, I cornered Mother's surgeon and pleaded with him to help me understand.

"Well, Pat," he stated matter-of-factly, "you see, your mother's skin has been damaged due to so many cobalt treatments. Working with her tissue is like trying to sew up Swiss cheese. We simply cannot force the stitches to hold together." He smiled patronizingly and assured me that no trace of cancer was found. "Perhaps," he added in his most professional voice, "in due time the drainage will stop, and the opening will heal."

A rush of fear and even anger gripped me. My thoughts could not compose a rational response to the doctor's prognosis. True, I was an adult, but at this moment I was reduced to the insecurity of a little girl. I ached to cry out for my mommy. Yet, Mother's strength was gone, and it was my turn to demonstrate courage. Determinedly, I opened my mouth to utter an intelligent word, but tears blurred my vision and choked my voice.

This may be your patient, I thought, *but she's my mother!* Reasonably, I knew it wasn't his fault, but I needed an outlet for my feelings. I found Dr. Keeley and spoke with him. He'd been my doctor as a child. Mother was still his patient, although he'd called in a specialist. He must have been disappointed too.

Touching my shoulder tenderly, he consoled, "Pat, you are worn out. You are mentally and physically exhausted. When your body gets in that condition, everything is amplified. Go home and get some rest."

Home? Yes. How long had I been here? Almost two weeks now? Relatives had taken over my duties with Dawn and Paige to allow me to be with Mother. I knew I had to gain my composure and go back into her room to say good-bye.

Gently, I pushed the door open and quietly walked to her bedside. Before I could speak a word she slowly turned her head toward me and reached out for my hand.

"Sug," she spoke in a whisper, "looks like you got here for the worst of it after all."

I swallowed back my tears and she sweetly advised, "You take my babies and go home to your husband. Gene needs you, too. I'll be all right . . . don't you worry."

I leaned over to kiss her good-bye. "I'll be back soon, Mom," was all I could get out. I left to pick up the girls, to pack, and drive home.

This would be the beginning of a stretched-out series of trips. I knew as soon as we were out of sight, Lee my stepfather would go immediately to the hospital. He wanted someone to be there constantly. A new love and respect for him was growing in me as I observed how faithfully and tenderly he cared for Mother. I felt ashamed as I remembered my earlier attitude toward their marriage.

As I drove home, I tried to analyze why I had been so skeptical of Mother's choice of a husband. George Lee Edwards had never been married before. He was from a large, very poor family that lived in the country. He worked as a carpenter, I surmised, because he had little formal education. He certainly wasn't handsome in my eyes, and I wondered what Mother saw in him. Perhaps she felt at ease with him because of her own childhood.

Mother was the third child born to Will and Bivie Adeline Johnson on November 18, 1919. Blond-haired, blue-eyed Mary Elizabeth would be the oldest daughter of six boys and three girls. I was told Grandma gave birth (at home) to sixteen children, although only nine lived to adult ages.

Grandpa eked out a living in the coal mines of Beech Creek, Kentucky. I knew Grandpa didn't spend much time in school because I remembered Grandma's proclaiming, "Why, I reckon I wuz the one who learnt' Daddy to read." Grandma was lovingly and dutifully by her husband's side whether he was planting a garden, grinding sausage, making soap, or 'tendin' church meetings. Each member of the family shared in the chores in order to survive.

Mother was forced to drop out of school in the eighth grade to help at home. Early in her teenage years she was attracted to a long-legged, brown-eyed boy named Merle Travis. His family lived nearby and the men folks were also coal miners.

These country dwellings were scattered in the woods a short distance from the main gravel road. It was not unusual to see a cluster of mailboxes at the end of the dirt path leading from these homes. Merle and Mary soon discovered this to be a convenient courtin' spot and met there regularly.

Their young love bloomed, and on April 12, 1937, at the tender ages of seventeen and nineteen, they married. Merle's father, fondly known as Uncle Rob, worried about how these two would make it financially. He was disappointed because his youngest son refused to work in the mines like his two older brothers, Taylor and John Melvin. Merle's only interest was his guitar. Sometimes he was even paid for playing at county fairs or school dances.

"Sister Bivie," Mr. Travis had addressed my grandmother, "I don't know how in the world that boy of mine will make a living for your girl. All in the world he knows how to do is pick that guitar."

Growing up in Muhlenberg County, Kentucky, etched a deep impression on the creative mind of Dad as a boy. His "Pappy," as he called his father, played a "rapping-style" banjo. When Dad was only eight years old he was imitating his Pappy on an old five-string banjo. His "Mammy" was a God-fearing woman who believed in the hickory stick and the Good

Book to raise children. When she sang, which was while working in the fields, scrubbing clothes on a washboard, or piecing
a quilt, her favorites were gospel songs such as "On Jordan's
Stormy Banks I Stand."

Like Mother, Dad also dropped out of the one-room schoolhouse in the eighth grade in Ebenezer. Dad inherited his older
brother, Taylor's, hand-built guitar at the age of twelve when
Taylor left for a factory job in Evansville, Indiana. Now where-
ever guitar music could be found, Dad was right in the middle.
He began to imitate and perfect the thumb-and-finger style
which he has become famous for today.

That influence later dominated his music. Songs like, "Kentucky Means Paradise," "Dark as a Dungeon," "Nine Pound
Hammer," and, of course, "Sixteen Tons," depicted his back-
ground. His perfected blend of folk ballads and unique guitar
style would make him a favorite with young and old.

As I drove toward Nashville my mind continued to retrace
the early lives of my parents. *Funny, the things we remember,*
I thought. Life now seemed so different and removed from what
it was then. It was hard to imagine the stories about the Great
Depression. Dad had talked about the days when there was no
money, and all they needed, such as overalls or a few yards of
cloth, was put on credit at the Beech Creek Company Store.

"Why, I bet that's where Dad came up with the words for
'Sixteen Tons'—'I owe my soul to the company store,' " I
chuckled out loud.

My mind lingered in the past as I wondered what it was like
when Mother and Dad married. Someone had told me about
Dad getting a job with a group called "Clayton McMichen and
His Georgia Wildcats." When he had a "real" job, he decided
to marry his childhood sweetheart. The only trouble was they
were too young, and Mary's father, Preacher Will, would never
give his consent. So Clayton McMichen, the famous fiddler,
stood up with them, making the ceremony legal.

I suppose Dad's big break came when he joined "The Drifting Pioneers" and became a regular on WLW Radio Station in Cincinnati, Ohio.

When it came time for my birth, I am told, Dad urged Mom to cross the Ohio border so his child would be born a Kentuckian. However, there wasn't time for such impetuous schemes. On March 25, 1939, Patricia Adeline Travis was born in Cincinnati. I inherited my grandmother's middle name, my Father's brown hair and eyes, and that undeniable Travis trait of oversized ears.

Faded pictures of a plump little girl nicknamed "Patty" with finger curls and ribbons serve as a reminder of our short-lived family days. Dad's success grew against the backdrop of an unfulfilled marriage which dissolved in divorce. On March 1, 1944, only weeks before my fifth birthday, Dad chose a path to Hollywood, California. Mother and I remained in Cincinnati.

I couldn't have been much older at that time than my own daughters are now, I calculated, jarring my thoughts to the present. I glanced at my little sleeping beauties in the backseat. *Why is it children look so angelic when they sleep?* I asked myself.

Highway 431 was a direct route between Nashville and Owensboro, and I was thankful. Gene had always assumed the responsibility of driving, because I'd never been good about figuring directions or reading maps. But in order to be with Mother I memorized this course well. I drove around courthouses and through sleepy towns like Central City, then Russellville, When I reached Springfield, I was in Tennessee, and my journey would soon end.

It was dusk now and just dark enough to turn on my headlights. The Nashville skyline came into view. I turned on the radio to break the silence. An all-too-familiar voice sang out,

> It's a nine pound hammer,
> It's a little too heavy,
> for my size, Honey, for my size.

I'm goin' on the mountain, goin' to see my baby,
But I ain't a comin' back.
Well, I ain't a comin' back.
Now roll on buddy, don't ya roll so slow.
Tell me how can I roll
when the wheels won't go.[4]

My heart began to pound unexplainably as it always did when I heard Dad's music. The disc jockey chattered enthusiastically. "Folks, you've just heard from Merle Travis, singing 'Nine Pound Hammer.' Nashville's proud to have Merle living back in the city of the Grand Ole Opry. If you want to hear more of his fine pickin' and singin', he'll be appearing tonight . . ."

Quickly, I turned off the station. I knew Dad had moved to Nashville. Uncle Kenneth, Mother's truck-driving brother, had talked with him at a truck stop recently and told me about their conversation. *Maybe,* I thought, *now that we're living in the same town he'll come see us.* Battling with myself, a sharp reprimand surfaced to remind me not to get my hopes up. *If he cares enough he'll come. In the meantime, I must forbid the pain from penetrating. Perhaps, if I keep denying the hurt it will go away.*

Dawn awoke and crawled over the seat to snuggle beside me. "Mommy, are we almost home?" she asked.

"Yes, Honey," I answered, brushing the tousled hair out of her eyes. I thought about Gene who would be waiting for us and felt a deep sense of thankfulness for him, not only as my husband, but also as a caring father to our daughters. Hugging Dawn closer to me, I assured her, ". . . and Daddy will be glad to see his girls."

NOTE

16

Prescription for Hope

"Mommy, I don't feel good," Dawn whimpered in a sleepy voice. She'd found her way to our bedroom and was standing by my side rubbing her eyes.

It was barely daylight and I ached for a few more hours of sleep. "Here, Honey, crawl under the covers by Mommy." I eased her quietly beside me, trying not to disturb Gene. Her little body was unusually warm. Touching her forehead I knew immediately she had fever.

"Come with me, Dawn," I forced myself out of bed. I hoped there was a bottle of baby aspirin in the medicine cabinet. There was. Maybe that would help. She was restless and didn't want to go back to bed. We curled up together on the couch and fell asleep.

"What are you two doing in here?" I looked up to see Gene standing in the doorway.

"Dawn doesn't feel good. I thought I'd call and get the name of Faye's pediatrician. Do you know his name?"

"No, but Faye and Richard think he's a good doctor. With five children, they should know. It's already seven," Gene said, glancing at the clock. "Why don't you call now? I imagine they're awake."

By this time, Paige, our three-year-old, had wandered in and was ready for breakfast. I poured her and Gene bowls of cereal and plugged in the coffee pot. Dawn wasn't hungry. I called my sister-in-law.

She listened as I described Dawn's symptoms. Faye's experienced voice was reassuring. She had such an easygoing manner. Her calm attitude always amazed me.

Faye's pediatrician was Dr. Dubuisson. He would work us in. I could leave Paige with Faye; Paige would enjoy going to Aunt Faye's, and it would make the office visit easier for me.

Dr. Dubuisson's nurse called me in after a short wait. She routinely filled out the necessary papers for a new patient.

The door opened, and I turned to see a smiling, chubby doctor appear. "Hello, young lady," he addressed Dawn. "How's Aunt Faye's niece? I bet you like playing with all those cousins." He chatted away as he examined Dawn, treating us like family friends. Instinctively, I liked this man. He seemed so kind and sensitive.

"Dawn, can you open your mouth great big for me?" Dr. Dubuisson coaxed. Quickly, he used the tongue depressor to look into her throat. "Just as I suspected," he announced. "Looks like a case of tonsillitis. I'll give you a prescription that should clear her up in no time," he said to me. "Check back with me in five days if she isn't better."

While the nurse prepared the room for the next patient, Dr. Dubuisson directed his attention to me. "I understand your mother is ill."

I was surprised he knew. Months had gone by, and Mother's condition had only worsened.

"Faye told me about her," he added. "How's she doing?"

"Well . . ." and I began describing the situation as best I could. Tears welled in my eyes. Dr. Dubuisson motioned for the nurse to take Dawn out so we could talk privately.

"They tell me Mother's skin tissue is so damaged from cobalt treatments her incision won't heal. She is just lying in her hospital bed with all this awful drainage coming through."

He looked at me thoughtfully, and I felt he understood. He called in his assistant.

"Listen to this," he requested, "and see if you don't think it

sounds like a case for Dr. Burrus." I repeated my story. They
nodded in agreement.

"Dr. Roger Burrus is a noted specialist in this field," emphasized Dr. Dubuisson. "Could you go see him if I call for an
appointment?"

Hope filled my heart. "Certainly," I answered without hesitation.

Dr. Dubuisson made a phone call. After a brief conversation
he told me I could go right now. He jotted down the name and
address and gave me brief directions. "Don't forget your prescription," he reminded.

I called Faye, and she offered to keep Dawn. I dropped her
off and rushed to the doctor's office. I was nervous and excited
as I walked in. Dr. Burrus was younger than I'd expected. He
listened intently, interrupting me occasionally.

Finally he began speaking, analyzing what I had reported
and offering advice. He ended by quietly saying, "If you will
bring your mother to see me, I will be glad to examine her and
see what I can do."

My heart sank. I knew Mother couldn't be moved, let alone
make the three-hour drive from Owensboro to Nashville. "Dr.
Burrus, there is no possible way she could travel this far in her
condition." My mind was spinning, and I couldn't lose the
opportunity to help her.

I swallowed, drew a deep breath, and could hardly believe I
had the nerve to ask, "Dr. Burrus, could you go see her in
Owensboro?" *How could I have made such a foolish request?
Why, doctors don't even make house calls anymore, let alone
drive 150 miles to see a potential patient! I was shocked by his
reply.*

"If you will get permission from your mother's physician, I
would be glad to," he answered.

"Oh, I will. You'll hear from me right away. Thank you.
Thank you very much!" I couldn't wait to tell Faye, to tell
Gene, to tell Lee, to tell Mother. There was hope. Today I had

not only received a prescription for a sore throat—but also a prescription for hope.

It wasn't long until Dr. Burrus made arrangements for Mother to be taken to Vanderbilt Hospital in Nashville. He believed that because she was such a young woman with other healthy organs, he could help her. He decided to perform a colostomy. I'd never heard the word and questioned him about it.

"A colostomy," Dr. Burrus explained in simple terms, "is when the intestine is directed through the abdominal wall. Her bowels will move into a small bag attached over the colostomy stoma. This should eliminate the drainage and give the opening in your mother's abdomen a chance to heal.

He must have noticed my grimace, because he hastened to explain, "Lots of people live long normal lives with colostomies. You probably have someone in your circle of acquaintances that has one without your even knowing it."

I wondered if that were possible. Mother accepted the idea and was eager to try. She had a strong will to get well. In September, 1966, the surgery was performed.

Her recuperation was slow. By the time she was released from the hospital, I had learned to help her attach the rubber bag to her side. The bag was held up by a belt that fit around her waist. It seemed uncomfortable and at times leaked. But gradually the opening did show signs of healing.

I knew Mother was happy to be out of the hospital and be back home. I continued making trips to be with her regularly. Dawn and Paige became Mam-ma's little helpers. They were good about being quiet when she needed sleep. "Sh-h-h-h" became a familiar sound as they warned each other with their fingers to their lips.

Everything appeared to be more peaceful until one afternoon shortly after lunch, I heard mother call my name from the bathroom. "Patty, come here! Quickly! Please!"

I rushed into the tiny bathroom to find her sitting bent over on the commode. "What's the matter, Mother?" I asked anxiously.

"Honey, I think I'm hemorrhaging; would you call Dr. Keeley? . . . and you'd better call Lee, too."

I did. Lee was home in minutes, and Dr. Keeley instructed us to meet him at Our Lady of Mercy Hospital.

When we arrived, the hospital staff ushered us right in. "Hello, Mary," they greeted her, "we've been missing you. Just can't stay away from this place, can you?" they teased. By now, she had been in and out so much they knew her on a first-name basis.

A pleasant looking nurse came with a wheelchair, and I walked beside Mom as we headed for the elevator. Lee stayed behind to sign the necessary admittance papers. I couldn't keep from chuckling when I heard Mom quip, "I don't know why the doctor doesn't just sew a zipper into me."

After a series of blood tests, two pints of B positive blood were ordered for a transfusion. "She has radiation cystitis," Dr. Keeley announced, "and that has caused the hemorrhaging. We'll need to keep her under observation for a few days."

A week later, I arrived at the hospital to find a well-dressed, white-haired lady talking with Mother. I stood at the door for awhile so I wouldn't interrupt. When Mother noticed me, she invited, "Come on in, Patty, there is someone here I want you to meet."

"Hello, I'm Mrs. Vance, a friend of your mother's from First Baptist Church," she introduced herself in a polite manner. "I remember you when you won the Kentucky Derby Queen contest." That seemed so long ago.

"Mary has been telling me all about your husband and children. She certainly is a proud grandmother," Mrs. Vance continued. I smiled modestly.

I also remember your father, Merle Travis. He was wonderful in that movie "From Here to Eternity" with Frank Sinatra,

Montgomery Clift, and Burt Lancaster. Didn't you just love it when he sang . . . ?"

"Re-enlistment Blues," I reminded her.

"Yes, that was it," she continued enthusiastically. "Your father played the part of a soldier. How long ago was that?" she asked.

"Wasn't that about 1953?" I asked mother.

She nodded "yes."

"Do you keep in touch with him," Mrs. Vance inquired innocently.

I quickly glanced at Mom, pausing to think of a tactful answer. Mother understood the hurt I felt and knew it was too deep to discuss. Her voice broke the silence, "Patty doesn't need her father like she used to. She has Lee now." Then almost to herself, she added, "But I always wanted Merle to love Patty."

I wished we could change the subject. Mrs. Vance kept talking, "What I came for was to tell Mary that I, too, have a colostomy. I don't want her to get discouraged."

How kind of this woman to share something so personal! My eyes scanned her body for visible signs of the surgery. I found none and felt a bit embarrassed.

"We colostomy patients must stick together," she remarked. "Now remember, Mary, don't give up." With that she spoke her good-byes and left.

"Mother, she was so nice. Have you known her long?"

"Yes," Mom answered, "but I'd never guessed she had a colostomy. She told me about a new lightweight bag that her Louisville doctor recommended. It's supposed to be more comfortable than the one I'm wearing and doesn't require a belt to hold it up. Maybe when I'm better, we could find out about it."

Oh, please Mother, do get better and I'll take you to that doctor in Louisville myself, I thought. *Why,* I wondered, *are some wounds so difficult to heal?*

17

I Prayed for Mother to Die

Tent dresses were "in," and Faye and I decided to go shopping. The Nashville Jaycees were having a banquet, and we wanted to dress in the latest fashion. Our husbands would be receiving awards at the dinner.

"How do you like this one?" I asked Faye, as I swirled, mimicking movie star Loretta Young sweeping from her dressing-room doorway.

Faye laughed. "Too bad these things weren't in style when we were pregnant!"

"I know," I giggled, scrutinizing my free-flowing frock in the mirror. It was a lovely color and certainly was comfortable. I glanced at the price tag and made my decision. "I'm going to buy this turquoise one," I announced to Faye. "I like that yellow one on you; it complements your red hair."

"OK," Faye grinned, "you talked me into it."

The shopping spree was fun. The change of pace from my hospital vigil was welcome. Gene had become involved with the Jaycees and thought it was a good avenue to meeting prospects for his insurance business. He was proud of his brother Richard for being their president and was following in his footsteps.

I went through the motions of having a good time at the banquet, but my heart wasn't in it. An after-hours party followed. There was a band and lots of booze. My head began to pound with the deafening music. The room was full of smoke. I wanted to go home.

Gene was talking with another couple and motioned for me to join him. "I want you to meet my wife," he put his arm around me trying to locate my waist in my new tent dress. "No, she's not pregnant," he informed the couple with a laugh.

"That's a pretty dress," remarked the wife of my husband's friend.

"Thank you," I replied smiling.

We forced a meaningless conversation while our husbands discussed business matters.

While driving home, I wondered why I couldn't enjoy these affairs like Gene did. *Maybe it was my state of mind,* I reasoned. I was too tired to think.

The next morning was Sunday. We dragged out of bed to attend church. Gene and I continued taking the girls, being true to the promise we'd made.

"Mommy, can I wear my new shoes?" Paige asked.

"You sure can, but be careful because they're slippery when they're new."

Dawn and Paige looked sweet dressed alike in pink ruffled dresses. I carefully tied their sashes.

Friendly faces greeted us as we walked into church. I looked at Gene; he was tall and handsome; Dawn and Paige were precious little girls. I was proud of our family. It made me feel good to be in church.

After leading the girls to their rooms for Sunday School, Gene and I went to the sanctuary. The organ was playing softly. A smiling gentleman offered us a bulletin, and we slipped into a pew near the back.

During the sermon, I glanced around at the well-dressed people. They seemed content, even serene. Did any of them have doubts? Did they ever argue with their husbands or yell at their children? Were any of them estranged from a father or fearful for a mother's life? They seemed so at home here.

"I can't wait to get out of this suit," Gene admitted after the service. He was loosening his tie as we headed toward our car. Dawn and Paige were practically running to keep up with their daddy's giant strides.

"Honey, what about stopping for a hamburger?" I suggested.

"Can we, Daddy? Can we?" the girls chimed in.

"Say please," he teased.

"Please, Daddy, please," they chorused.

"OK," Gene surrendered, "looks like I'm outnumbered, but after lunch we're all taking a nap." That statement wasn't met with quite as much enthusiasm.

Monday morning Gene helped me pack the car. It was time to visit Mother again. He waved good-bye as we headed for the familar route along Highway 431 to Kentucky.

The sun broke the chill of the cool fall morning. The girls were in a playful mood, and I improvised games to keep them busy. We counted cows as we drove past farmland. We sang songs they'd learned in Sunday School. "Deep and wide, deep and wide," they stretched their arms, demonstrating the words. "There's a fountain flowing deep and wide."

"You'll have to sing that one for your Great-grandma Johnson. She'll be at Pap-pa's house to take care of you-all," I explained.

"Will she make me some dumplings?" Dawn asked.

"Yes, I'm sure she will. You like Grandma's chicken and dumplings, don't you?"

"Yum, yum," she answered, licking her lips.

There was always family or friends to take care of my children while I stayed with Mother. I was grateful I didn't have to worry about their care.

As we pulled into the driveway, I saw Grandma in the back yard hanging up clothes. Rubbing her hands on her apron, she came to the car to greet us. "Patty, Honey, your Mother will be so glad to see you. Now don't worry about me and them girls; you hurry right over to the hospital. We'll have some chicken and dumplings ready when you get back and Lee comes home from work."

Sometimes I wondered where my seventy-year-old grandmother found so much energy. Of course, had I asked her, she'd come back with, "Why, Honey, it's the Lord. He gives me my strength."

I gave the girls a quick hug and reminded them to be good while I was gone. Sometimes I felt guilty for being away from them so much.

As I drove to the hospital, the autumn leaves glistened in the bright sunlight. *I wish Mother could enjoy this beautiful day with me. She must get tired of those stark white hospital room walls.*

Cars crowded the parking lot at Our Lady of Mercy Hospital. I had arrived during visiting hours. Finally I found a parking place and walked through the familiar lobby to the elevator.

When I came to Mother's room, I hesitated at the door. Her pastor, Dr. David Nelson, was praying with her. He visited Mother faithfully. He'd hold her hand in his as they prayed together. I wondered if God would hear those prayers and make her well. The pastor nodded for me to come in as he slipped out. I tiptoed in. The strong odor in the room was difficult to accept. Mother's condition was demoralizing and inhumane. She lay flat on her back because even the colostomy failed to help the open wound to heal. The bowel had found the place of least resistance and had erupted through the skin. The strong acid in the gastric juices was eating away at the skin around the wound, causing an angry redness. I tried to disguise the smell with spray deodorants for the room and perfume for her. Nothing worked.

As I looked down at her I thought, *It's hard to imagine when we are young and healthy that anything like this could possibly happen.*

Mom's painful eyes stared up at me from her hospital bed. "Sug," she mumbled through the influence of pain-killing drugs, "You wouldn't think a human being could live in this condition."

Her remark wasn't a sign of self-pity, or a question, but simply a statement of observation. I forced a weak smile and searched for some cheerful words. I, too, wondered how long she could go on like this. I automatically picked up an emesis basin in one hand and a syringe in the other to suction the secretions from the open wound in her abdomen.

It wasn't as if she were old. Mom was still in her forties. But then, cancer knows no age limits or boundaries of destruction.

As a young mother, I was well aquainted with the task of changing diapers. I had accepted the fact that babies don't always smell of talcum powder and baby oil. I knew how to treat diaper rash and to recognize a sour tummy. All these matters became routine with little ones, but the odor in Mother's room this day was the smell of death.

Each succeeding trip I made to care for Mother became increasingly difficult. *How long must this continue?* Since Gene had been promoted to a position that moved us to Memphis, the drive now required five hours. I was growing weary.

Mother slept on a sheepskin to prevent bedsores. It was becoming almost impossible to find a place to give her a shot. Nurses tried injecting her medication through veins in her ankles. Someone stayed with her around the clock.

Late one evening, when it was my turn to spend the night, her faint whisper startled me. I strained to hear.

"Patty," she mumbled.

"Yes, Mom, what is it?"

"I hear my daddy singing."

She waited for my response. I didn't know how to answer.

"Patty, do you hear him? He's in the next room." Urgently, she insisted I go and check on him.

Reluctantly, I obeyed, stepping out into the hall for a moment. For years growing up with Grandpa I'd heard his voice rise in praise, singing gospel hymns, but Pa had been dead for years. *Was Mother hallucinating or could God be giving her a glimpse into heaven? Did He do things like that?*

When I returned to her room she was asleep. Sitting beside the bed, I could hear her labor for her next breath. Her chest rose and fell in her frail body. Her stomach was distended and swollen like pictures I'd seen of malnourished children. It was hard to believe she was my mother.

Why hadn't God healed her? Why must she suffer like this? I clenched my teeth to fight back locked-in emotions. My head bowed forward and rested in my hands. An unspoken prayer fell silent on my lips. "Oh, Dear God, I love her so much. I can't stand to see her suffer anymore. If You can't make her well, then please just take her on with You."

My face and hands were wet with tears when I raised my head. The night struggled into dawn, and Lee came to relieve me.

The cold February winds chilled me as I hurried to my car. I looked forward to collapsing under warm quilts. Grandma would have a bed turned down for me. I was pleased Dawn and Paige had stayed with their Aunt Faye this trip. I was totally exhausted.

No sooner had I dozed off from fatigue than the loud ring of the telephone startled me. How many times had I been alarmed by the phone? The fear of that final call always lingered. I staggered to answer.

"Hello, Yes, this is Mary Edwards's daughter," I muttered. "Yes, I'll be there right away."

I threw on some clothes and rushed to the hospital. The parking lot was nearly empty. I hurried through the back emergency entrance to save time. *Why was the elevator taking so long?* I raced down the long corridor. People were already gathered outside Mother's room. I looked into the eyes of my favorite nurse. She'd been crying. Lee came to meet me.

"She's gone," he announced calmly. "She's gone." I felt his big arm around my shoulders.

Thank God, I thought. *Thank God! She's out of her misery.* I walked over to her lifeless body. I wanted to touch it, but I couldn't.

"Finally, Mother, you don't have to suffer anymore. You've been a good soldier."

So many times before she'd answered that statement with, "Maybe so, but I'm getting tired of marching." She didn't have to march anymore.

I dropped coins in the pay phone down the hall and waited for Gene's voice. I glanced around the hospital surroundings that were so familar to me. Helping care for Mother during this time, I had earned the freedom to go into the linen closet or nurses' station with no restrictions. Now, I was no longer needed. I wanted to leave this place and never return.

Why isn't Gene answering?

"Hello," I heard my husband's sleepy voice at last.

"Gene," I rasped, trying not to cry, "Mother is dead."

"Honey, are you all right?" he asked.

"Yes, I'm fine. Can you come right away? . . . I don't know whether you should bring the girls or not. Maybe it would be better to let them stay in Nashville with Faye.

"I'll be with you tonight," Gene assured me.

"OK," I managed.

I hung up and went to the private room the hospital provides for the bereaved. A reporter was taking notes of information from Lee for the newspaper.

"How long was she ill?" I heard the reporter ask.

I thought to myself, *It's been over two years and six major operations.*

Lee answered all the routine questions, and the interview ended. We were now free to leave. It was over. I sleepwalked through the rest of the day.

Opening the *Messenger–Inquirer* newspaper the next morning, I turned to the obituary column. I spotted Mother's name, Mrs. George Lee Edwards. The article read as follows:

Mrs. Mary Elizabeth Edwards, 48, of 104 Byers Avenue died at 7:45 a.m. Wednesday, February 28, 1968, in Our Lady of

Mercy Hospital after an illness of 30 months. She was a General Electric employee and a member of AFL-CIO Local 738.

Born at Beech Creek, Kentucky, on November 18, 1919, she had lived in Owensboro since 1948 and was a member of the First Baptist Church.

Surviving are her husband, George Lee Edwards; a daughter, Mrs. Gene Eatherly, and two grandchildren; her mother, Mrs. Bivie Johnson; six brothers, Arley, Elgie, Bobby, Kenneth, Lelan, and Paul Johnson, and two sisters, Mrs. Glodean Hester and Mrs. Lois Jenkins.

Services will be held at 1:30 p.m. Friday at the James H. Davis Funeral Home conducted by Rev. David Nelson, pastor of the First Baptist Church. Burial will be in Pleasant Hill Cemetery.

Someone made arrangements for Mother's funeral. Flowers arrived until the room was full. I was overwhelmed that so many came to offer condolences. Even Dad's brother, Uncle Taylor, and his family came to express their sympathy. These loving friends and relatives helped ease my pain of grief. I secretly longed for some acknowledgement from my father, but there was none.

Gene was a source of comfort. He chose to leave Dawn and Paige with Faye and Richard in Nashville. I wondered if later I would regret their not being included. Dying is natural, and children can't always be shielded from reality. But at their young ages of three and five perhaps it was best. Their memories of her are strange and sweet. Dawn remembers taking Mam-ma her pills and buttermilk. Mother's doctor couldn't stand buttermilk and always declared, "Mary, you can swallow anything if you can swallow buttermilk."

Paige remembers how Mam-ma would tie coins in the corner of a handkerchief when Aunt Lois took her to Sunday School.

I will always recall one special flower arrangement at her funeral. It was in the shape of a wheel. There were nine spokes and one was broken. Mother's brother Elgie designed it to symbolize her family. Six spokes were covered with blue carnations to represent the boys, and three spokes were covered with pink carnations to represent the girls. The broken pink spoke was in memory of Mother. It was touching and meaningful in the sea of flowers.

18

Premiums of Love

Accepting the death benefit from Mother's life insurance policy was difficult. Lee and I were to share $10,000 equally. Fortunately, hospitalization had adequately covered the expense during her illness.

I thought about Mother's former job at the General Electric Tube Plant. She'd been an assembly line worker, welding TV tube wires together. There had been times when my demands must have been thoughtless. If I had wanted a new sweater or winter coat, I had usually gotten my way, even when she couldn't afford it. How many times had I heard her say, "Patty, we just barely have enough to make ends meet"? Now what right did I have to claim any compensation for my inconsiderate and selfish behavior as a child?

I thought about Lee. *I'm thankful she's had him by her side the last twelve years. Lee restored balance and brought happiness into her life. Perhaps I should offer my portion of the money to him.*

Guilt rooted in my heart as scenes of the past paraded through my mind. My moving to California to live with Dad must have been a difficult time for Mother, but she hadn't tried to hold me back. Now that she was gone it became so clear that she had valued my happiness more than her own.

Once while living in California, I had received a letter from Aunt Lois, Mother's youngest sister. She had reminded me that Mother was growing older and needed me. That had brought a chuckle from Dad, and rightfully so . . . Mom had just turned forty. Who could have known her life would end at forty-eight?

All these years I had taken her for granted. She had always been there when I needed her. I had planned to express more appreciation and love to her—someday. Now it was too late.

I desperately longed to talk with someone who had known and loved Mother as I had. Mother's brother, Uncle Kenneth, came to my mind, because she had often turned to him.

Uncle Ken was the strong one in the Johnson family, always helping others. When I was a little girl he'd been a father figure to me. Now he was father to four sons and one daughter. He earned a good living for them as a truck driver. Even though Uncle Ken may have appeared tough, I saw only tenderness in his soft blue eyes.

As I began to explain my turmoil to him, I knew he understood. Calmly, in his simple demeanor, he said, "Patty, your mother wouldn't want you feeling this way, and neither would Lee. She loved you and worked hard for you all her life. She always wanted nice things for you."

Tears burned my eyes as I listened. *Yes, she wanted so much for me. She'd given all she could. How could I refuse to accept? I couldn't.*

I knew immediately how I would use my part of her insurance money. It would go toward buying a house. That would please her. Mother had always longed for a place of her own and never had one until she and Lee married.

I recalled how happy she was for Gene and me when we had bought our first house in Tucson. Mother had been able to identify with the difficulty of our financial situation. She'd expressed those feelings in a letter she'd written after the children were born. It read:

> I am happy to have a wonderful son-in-law to take care of and love all my babies, and I'm sure he is loved in return. I'm so happy with Gene because he is so thoughtful of the things you need. I know it hasn't been easy with

two sweet babies and a home. I only wish I was rich so I
could pay it off for you.

Most of the money from selling our Tucson home had been
swallowed up in moving and living expenses. Once again, we
were living in a rented house. I felt good about my decision. The
desire she had expressed in her letter, "I only wish I was rich
so I could pay it off for you," would partially become a reality.
This was only the beginning of finding myself making choices
and doing what I felt would be pleasing to Mother.

In November, 1968, seven months after her death, we moved
into our newly built 2,400-square-foot dream home. It was a
white brick contempory style with a vaulted ceiling and stairs
leading to a balcony which overlooked the living room. The
see-through fireplace serviced both the living room and den. We
included every extra imaginable from an intercom to a unique
built-in vacuum system which upped the price to nearly
$30,000. We were proud of our house.

While we heard many neighbors talking about a fear of being
transferred, we confidently boasted, "Not us—we're going to
live here the rest of our lives."

The first Christmas in our new home, Lee came to visit for
the holidays. I wasn't sure how our relationship would be after
Mother's death. However, after our Christmas together, those
uncertainties melted away. He was "Pap-pa" to our children.
Although Lee didn't express his feelings verbally, they were
made known by his every action. The most revealing insight
was when he choked back the tears as he told us good-bye.

Dawn and Paige questioned, "Mommy, why does Pap-pa
cry?" How could I tell them the tears were for the woman he
loved? They were for my mother, their grandmother, who was
no longer here to express her love. He was trying to do that for
her. We were his family, and nothing could change that fact.

I had every reason to be happy in our new luxury home, but
I wasn't. The distress inside me continued. Sometimes I found

myself crying for no apparent reason. In my new neighborhood there was no one who understood what I had just gone through. I'll never forget one late afternoon when I was alone. The sky turned dark with rain clouds, and sudden, deafening claps of thunder burst through my thoughts. I retreated to my upstairs bedroom like a frightened child. I lay down across the bed, cuddling my pillow close to me. Haunting memories of the Pleasant Hill Cemetery flooded my mind. *Poor Mother,* I imagined, *is cold and all alone in her grave.* Of course, I knew better. I suppressed the desire to cry out, "I want my mommy."

Why wouldn't the pain of her death go away? Sometimes I wanted to scream for help but to whom? I ached for comfort. Deep inside I allowed myself to believe that Dad would come to me and express belated sympathy for my loss. But he didn't. Surely I could learn to cope with these emotions.

Mrs. Ruby Harris, an elderly Sunday School teacher from Eudora Baptist Church, began to visit me as a prospect for her class. After some persuasion, I agreed to attend. After all, we were now members of Eudora. I hadn't participated in Bible study before, and I was embarrassed about my slowness in finding certain Scriptures. When we had a time of prayer, I was always the first to bow (or I should say, duck?) my head for fear of being called on to voice the prayer.

I'd never had the courage to request prayer for Mother during her illness. *Is God punishing me because I haven't been obedient?* I wondered.

One Sunday after listening to a member's prayer for an illness in her family, I nearly exploded inside. Tearfully, I confessed to the class about Mother's death and the torment I couldn't escape. (I wasn't yet ready to admit openly the struggle I felt with Dad.)

That afternoon Mrs. Harris loaned me a book to read about God's will. It only added to my confusion. I reasoned, *Why pray? It doesn't seem to make any difference. God is going to do whatever He wants to anyway.*

I couldn't quiet the doubts and questions that stirred within my mind. Questions like, if there is a God, how could He allow such suffering in this world? If there is a God and prayer is real, why didn't He hear Dr. Nelson's prayers and heal my mother? Did God even hear those prayers at all? Why God? Why? Why? Why?

I decided to write to Dr. Fred Wood, the pastor of Eudora Baptist Church. I unloaded my questions on him.

His reply brought some peace to my troubled heart.

It is not easy to watch our loved ones suffering. We live in a body, and sometimes it seems the soul is just not ready or willing to leave the body. The relationship between the body and the soul is a mysterious one. There have been times when I have felt that it would have been far better if the person could go on and leave the body and depart to be with the Lord. Paul says that "to be absent from the body is to be present with the Lord." This is the simplest, and yet the most comforting, explanation I know of to be found anywhere.

Sometimes it seems the body just will not give up the spirit and had rather suffer physical pain than release the soul to its onward flight to God. Because we are human and limited in knowledge, we pray for our loved ones. We want God to leave them with us as long as it is best, but sometimes deep in our hearts we know it is best for that loved one to leave the body.

What is the answer to our suffering and problems?

There is no answer to the mind. It is an answer of the heart. You remember the story of Job. His friends tried to explain to him why he was suffering. One by one they proposed certain intellectual reasons. Job, however, could answer each one of these. It was only when God spoke to him that he was satisfied. As you read the chapters which contain God's speeches to Job, you see that God never did actually explain to Job the reason for his suffering. He merely assured Job that He was present with him. This satisfied Job. So, I think it is the same with our suffering today.

We can never have an academic answer. We can only be assured that God is with us and loves us. When we are fully and completely convinced of God's love, faith can take over, and we then are assured that whatever happens God will use it to further His purposes for our lives. We learn things in suffering. Our tears can become telescopes by which we can see more clearly that God is at work in our lives, even during the crushing periods of sorrow.

Dr. Wood's letter included a poem by Robert Browning:

> I walked a mile with Pleasure
> She chattered all the way
> But left me none the wiser
> For all she had to say.
>
> I walked a mile with Sorrow
> And ne'er a word said she
> But, oh the things I learned from her
> When Sorrow walked with me!

Dr. Wood's words made sense to me. I appreciated his letter and referred to it often. Perhaps I was beginning to catch a glimpse of light in the darkness of my soul.

19

Hello Texas—Good-bye Tennessee

"Daddy's home, Daddy's home," Dawn and Paige squealed with delight as they raced into the kitchen to announce his early arrival.

"Hi, Honey," I greeted Gene. I pulled the last batch of chocolate chip cookies from the oven. "What are you doing home so early?"

"Can I have another one, Mommy, please?" Dawn interrupted, holding out her hand.

"Me, too," Paige echoed.

"OK." I quickly stacked a bunch of warm cookies on a paper plate and suggested that the girls play outside.

"Gene, is something wrong?" I questioned, wiping my hands on the dish towel.

"Sit down a minute." His earnest look drew my attention. "Remember a couple of years ago when I told you about World Heritage Life merging with Service Life in Fort Worth, Texas?"

"Yes," I answered, puzzled by his delayed concern.

"Due to the merger," Gene went on, taking a deep breath as if to give him strength to finish his sentence, "they are phasing out my sales division in Tennessee."

He searched my face for a hint of reaction, then continued, "They've offered me a management position in the home office."

I gave my mind time to absorb this unexpected news. "You mean we would have to move to Texas?"

"Yes."

I looked around my freshly wallpapered kitchen with its

matching avocado appliances. *How can I leave this house? I thought; the new hasn't even worn off. We haven't even lived in it for one year. I can still remember visiting day after day as it was being built. It'll be like leaving a child I've watched grow from birth.*

Before I could form my thoughts into words, Gene gave me a hug, grabbed a cookie, and gushed, "You'll like Texas, just you wait and see. Everything will work out all right."

Through the haze that clouded my mind, I knew he was trying to be cheerful. Gene was good at looking for the positive side of every situation.

Then, as if it were any normal day, he asked, "Will I have time to mow the lawn before supper?" He was already bounding upstairs to change from his business suit into his work clothes.

Filling the sink with warm, sudsy water, I began to clean up my cookie mess so I could start dinner. I swallowed back the lump in my throat and stared out the kitchen window into the backyard.

That night after the children were tucked into bed, Gene and I stayed up talking. We decided to sell the house ourselves. Gene wouldn't have to start his new job in Texas until January 1970. Since this was only the middle of the summer of '69, we deceived ourselves into thinking we had plenty of time.

Time didn't adjust itself to suit our schedule, however. Even though we had put our house on the market in early November, the deadline came for Gene to leave, and it still hadn't sold. The inevitable was obvious. The girls and I would stay and wait for a buyer. Gene would move into the Worth Hotel in downtown Fort Worth. He could walk directly across the street to his office at World Service Life Insurance Company.

January was a terrible month to consider moving. The "FOR SALE" sign appeared as lonely on the dead, drab grass as I felt inside. The frequent long-distance phone calls from Gene helped a little.

The most interest in our advertisement for "Dream House for Sale" came from real-estate brokers. One morning a cheerful, well-dressed young man appeared on my doorstep. "Mrs. Eatherly," he smiled, "I would like to talk to you about listing your home."

I listened to his sales pitch with forced politeness. Casually, before leaving he included, "Mrs. Eatherly, I am a Christian, and I want you to know I pray about every house I sell. Also, I can promise you I will treat you as fairly as if you were my very own sister."

Although I didn't list my house with him, I thought his approach was most unusual.

Keeping the house in order became a tedious task. "Girls," I nagged Dawn and Paige, "can't you please help Mommy keep the house clean?" I knew I was growing irritable with this intrusion in my life. "Don't leave your skates on the sidewalk. Hang your coats up. Put your toys away. Don't use those fresh towels. No, I can't bake cookies!" I constantly felt pressured to keep the house spotless in case there were an opportunity to show it.

Finally, that long-awaited day arrived. A couple that was being transferred to Memphis made an offer on the house. Gene spoke to the man long distance. Arrangements were made for them to purchase our house for $33,500. They would have occupancy on March 1, 1970.

Part of me could relax, while part of me realized the pressure was on to find a place to live in Fort Worth. I made plans to leave Dawn and Paige with my next-door neighbor and fly to Texas.

"Mommy, will there be lots of horses and cowboys in Texas?" the children asked as my dear friend, Mary Kate Grimm, drove me to the airport. I was thankful for her help during this ordeal.

"Dawn and Paige will be fine; you enjoy being with Gene,"

Mary Kate encouraged. "Laurie and Chip are excited to have them staying with us."

Our families had grown close living next door to each other. I knew we would miss them.

"Don't bother coming in," I suggested as we drove to the airport entrance. It seemed easier that way.

"Bye, girls, give Mommy a hug. Now be sweet, and have fun while I'm gone," I added.

I turned to Mary Kate, "Wish me luck in finding a house."

They drove away waving.

"Flight 323, now boarding at gate number twelve for Dallas, Texas," boomed the amplified voice over the PA system. I hurried to find my way as we were herded to our seats. *Funny, I thought, this used to be so routine when I was a stewardess, and now I am the unfamilar passenger.*

Once we were airborne I searched for the release button on my stiff upright seat. I pushed forcefully and tilted back to try and relax. I was drawn into a deep wave of thoughts as a sea of uncertainties about the future tossed in my head.

In an unbelievable one hour and ten minutes, Gene and I were together in Texas. I had almost forgotten the advantages of jet travel. Rushing through the crowded airport, we soon claimed my luggage and headed for downtown Fort Worth.

"Wait until you see my bachelor pad," Gene teased. We soon arrived at the Worth Hotel on West Seventh Street. When we stopped, I looked up and read a banner stretched across the street. "WELCOME TO THE 74th ANNUAL SOUTH-WESTERN EXPOSITION AND FAT STOCK SHOW."

We hurried out of the cold into a lobby crowded with men who looked like honest-to-goodness cowboys. "What's going on here?" I asked Gene.

"There's a livestock show and a big indoor rodeo at a place called Will Rogers Memorial Center," he answered. "I'm told it's one of the biggest events of the year. Maybe we can go sometime," Gene suggested.

I couldn't keep from laughing. "Why are you laughing?" Gene asked quizzically.

"When I left, Dawn and Paige asked if there were lots of cowboys and horses in Fort Worth. It seemed like such a preposterous question. I can't wait to tell them about this!"

The following morning after an early breakfast Gene and I met with a realtor. She patiently drove us all over Fort Worth to look at houses. Before the day was over we made an offer on a contemporary-style house in the southwest area. There was an offer ahead of ours that would have first priority, but our realtor told us she would do all she could and let us know.

The next day Gene had to work, and I waited for a call. In the stillness of the quiet hotel room I began thinking about the young man who tried to list our home in Memphis. His idea of praying came to my mind. It seemed rather absurd to me that God cared about such minor matters, but the desire to pray took root in my heart. Skeptically, I breathed a prayer for God to lead us to the place where He would want our family to live.

The phone rang. "Hello," I answered. It was the realtor. In our brief conversation, I learned that the owners had accepted the first offer. I thanked her for her trouble and hung up.

Gene planned to get off work early so I finished dressing, knowing we would begin our search again. The calm sense of assurance I experienced was unnatural to my normal disposition.

The phone rang again.

"Hello."

"Hi, Honey, how's it going?" Gene asked.

Before I could answer, Gene continued, "Are we the proud owners of a Texas house?"

"No," I had to admit.

"No?" he repeated unbelieving.

I explained what had happened. He suggested I buy a newspaper and circle some places we could look into.

When Gene arrived at the hotel, I was eager to go. There was one place that sounded especially interesting in a suburb called Wedgwood. It was for sale by the owner, but we couldn't make an appointment to see it until eight that evening. We drove around many areas of town investigating the advertisements I'd circled in the *Star Telegram* classified ads section. One by one we checked them off.

"It sure would have made things easier if they'd taken our offer on the one house we really liked. This is hard work," Gene confessed.

"Now, don't get discouraged. I just know we're going to find something good," I said.

"Let's stop for a bite to eat, then go to our eight o'clock appointment," Gene suggested.

We felt a bit more optimistic after taking time to relax. Now to find a street called Wrigley Way in Wedgwood.

Every street in Wedgwood appeared to begin with a W. According to our map, this house should be located between Waco and Walla right off Wedgmont Circle. We almost gave up before we finally found it. Again we checked the address before getting out of the car. Yes, this was 6052. It looked good on the outside, a white-brick-and-rock combination. We opened a decorative iron gate to a beautifully landscaped court-yard. Gene knocked on the door, giving me a wink as I shivered in the chilly January wind.

"You must be the Eatherlys," we were greeted at the door. "I'm Alex Eastus and this is my wife Christine. Come on in out of the cold."

A fire was blazing in the oversized fireplace. Two big easy chairs faced it, and the stereo played soft music.

"What a nice-sized den," I remarked.

"It is unusually large," Alex Eastus responded, "measures 15′ × 22′. We've always loved this room."

"The ceiling is quite unique, too," Christine added. Our attention was drawn to the arched dome-like structure which had a sparkle effect that glittered in the firelight.

Gene and I looked at each other across the room with a secret smile of approval. *Now, if only the rest of the house is equally as pleasing.* It was. Gene and I were both satisfied with the floor plan of 2,400 square feet.

Christine said, "If you don't mind stepping out into the cold, there is something I would like to show you in the backyard." She turned on the outdoor lights. There was the most adorable little girl's playhouse I'd ever seen. Flower boxes were built underneath the windows, and there was a miniature door sized just right for our five- and six-year-old girls.

Hurrying back into the den, we sat down and began talking business. They were asking $32,500 at a 5 1/4 percent interest rate. Alex was a lawyer and would handle all the legal transactions, saving us money.

Before we left that evening we had agreed on most of the necessary arrangements. As an extra bonus we learned that J. T. Stephens Elementary School was only three blocks down the street. Everything seemed perfect.

Gene and Alex shook hands at the door, each seemingly satisfied.

As we drove away I remembered my prayer and whispered a silent "Thank you." God had not only heard, but He cared and He answered!

20

Pearls from Pain

Mrs. Allred, the school secretary, shuffled through the papers to transfer Dawn and Paige to J. T. Stephens Elementary School. "Everything seems to be in order," she said, glancing at the girls. "I have your report cards and medical records. If you'll just have a seat in our principal's office, he'll be right with you." She gestured to the open room across the hall.

We walked into the book-lined office, and I sat down in a hard wooden chair facing a worn desk. The girls nestled as close to me as possible. They were unusually quiet and still.

A friendly-looking man in a brown suit entered. He casually introduced himself, "Mrs. Eatherly, I'm Mr. Jones, the principal." Comfortably relaxed in his chair, he continued, "I understand your daughters will be new students with us."

"Yes," I responded. "We just moved here from Memphis, Tennessee."

Tilting back slightly in his swivel chair he asked, "What grade are you girls in?"

They hesitated with that desperate, "You-tell-him,-Mom" look on their faces.

"Dawn is in the first grade, and Paige is in kindergarten," I answered for them. I could almost feel their hearts pounding.

"My secretary will get you assigned to your teachers. I hope you will be very happy here," Mr. Jones concluded politely.

Mrs. Allred appeared with an enrollment form for me to sign. As I was completing the form, I heard her tell Dawn, "You will be in Mrs. Denton's class. And Paige, you will be assigned to Mrs. Gilbert."

They gave her weak, shy smiles.

We followed Mrs. Allred down the hall. She first stopped at the kindergarten room. I quickly scanned the class of freshly scrubbed five-year-olds. Their angelic little faces turned to see the new student. Paige stood frozen beside me.

The teacher took her by the hand, "We're so glad to have you, Paige."

"Bye, Honey, I'll be right here to pick you up as soon as school is over." I forced myself not to look back.

Dawn's room was only a short distance away. Since she was the big sister, she pretended to be brave. I sensed she didn't want any display of affection that might embarrass her. She looked up and said, "See you after school, Mom."

Walking the few blocks home, I wondered what life would be like living in Fort Worth. It was the middle of March, and I was grateful for the spring-like weather. *Dawn and Paige will enjoy walking to and from school,* I reasoned, *when they meet new friends.* I could empathize with their going into those strange classrooms today. Meeting new people isn't always easy for children or adults.

How would I adjust? Before moving I remembered a suggestion about making new friends in the church. That seemed like sound advice. With the girls settled in school, perhaps finding a church should come next.

I thought about the going-away party my Memphis Sunday School class had given me. They had presented me with a book and also a personal note from each member. I walked home, wondering if I could find those letters. It seemed important to read them again now.

As soon as I reached home, I began searching. I found the book and the notes with a stack of books waiting to be placed on the empty shelves in the den. I sat down in the quiet clutter and began to read.

The first note was from my sweet teacher, Mrs. Ruby Harris. Her message read:

February 18, 1970

Dear Pat,

I am grateful that I had the privilege of having you in my class.

I shall always remember your thoughtful, kind attitude towards other people. Also your love for your mother. She must have been a wonderful person to rear a daughter like you.

Your interest in Bible study was a challenge to me. May you find another church home soon.

Sincerely,

Ruby Harris

I felt unworthy of her compliments. I reread each note carefully and felt encouraged by them.

Several notes were almost like reading someone's prayer. One member ended her message to me with: "May God lead you into a new place in your new home and make you contented and happy."

"May God lead you," rolled over and over in my mind. Was God leading? It did seem ironic how we had moved from Arizona to Tennessee during the period of time when Mother needed me most and then after her death transferred to Texas.

I pulled my legs up under me, leaned my head back, and closed my eyes. *It seemed God had led us to this house,* I thought. I recalled praying about our house.

I found myself timidly praying that God would guide us to the right "church home," as my Sunday School teacher had suggested.

He did. After visiting several churches in the area we joined Southcliff Baptist Church. Frank Minton was the pastor at the time. His former baseball pitching career captured Gene's attention. He often used unique illustrations from his experiences and cleverly titled a revival we attended "Sermons on the Mound." He had also published a book entitled *Baseball's Ser-*

mon on the Mound. Gene could identify with this preacher's athletic ability and personality.

"Brother Minton," as his congregation called him, subtly directed our attention and interest to God's Word. We soon enrolled as members of the church and the Sunday School. Gene began meeting some of the men by joining Southcliff's softball team.

I visited an organization called Round Table suggested by my new Sunday School teacher, Mary Jane White. This attractive lady wasn't much older than I, but she had a deep commitment to Bible study and teaching her class. She seemed so comfortable when she prayed . . . as if she were talking to her best friend.

The Round Table meeting was held in Mary Jane's elegantly decorated home. There was an immediate warmth among the women. Each furnished a covered dish for a luncheon which followed a book review. Dozens of books were displayed on a table. After the review the ladies eagerly examined them. The purpose of Round Table, I speculated, was to spark an interest in Christian literature.

I'd never been much of a reader and had the mistaken idea that Christian books were dull. Simply to appear sociable, I went to the table and curiously looked over the selection. Intentionally I chose the skinniest book on the table. It was entitled *Games Husbands and Wives Play* by John W. Drakeford (Broadman Press). *Surely I could get through this one,* I thought. The title was intriguing.

"Mary Jane," I asked, "May I take this one to read?"

"Certainly," she answered. "You'll love Dr. Drakeford."

I certainly didn't want to confess that I hadn't heard of him.

"By the way," I questioned, "How do you join this group?" I thought this would be an excellent way to meet some new friends.

"You just did," she smiled, "by checking out a book."

That was the beginning of a growing thirst for Christian literature that has never been quenched. Not only did I begin to meet new friends from our church, but I also met new friends through reading. My list of admired authors grew, and so did my understanding of applying the Scriptures to my life. Testimonies of people whose lives had been changed because of their courage to trust God became my favorites. Some of these people were famous, such as Catherine Marshall, Dale Evans Rogers, Ethel Waters, and Francis and Edith Schaeffer. Some were ordinary people like me.

Books like Catherine Marshall's *To Live Again* were exactly what I needed to help me handle my grief. She taught me to think of the date Mother died as her "Heavenly Birthdate." That is how she referred to Peter Marshall's, her husband's, day of death.

Quite honestly, I was still struggling with my sense of guilt. The peace I read about in other people's lives was absent from mine. There was a constant tug-of-war going on between my head and my heart. I wanted to be free of this, but I didn't know how.

The book, *How to Be a Christian Without Being Religious,* focused my attention on how we should never stop paying our debt of love. This book by Fritz Ridenour was a study of the New Testament Book of Romans. It reminded me of the kindness and love shown Mother by her friends and family in Kentucky.

Had I properly expressed my gratitude to these people? I doubt it. Perhaps a note of thanks to Mother's pastor would ease my conscience. I sat down and typed the following letter to him:

April 28, 1970

Dear Dr. Nelson,
    I've just finished reading *How to Be a Christian Without Being Religious.* The point in the book that hit me right

between the eyes was we should never stop paying our debt of love. This thought came from Romans 13:10, which says, "Love worketh no ill to his neighbor: therefore love is the fulfilling of the law."

When I thought about this verse, I couldn't help thinking about your kindness to my mother, Mary Edwards. Of course, this isn't the first time I've thought about it, but I felt I must tell you how very grateful I am to you and the people in the church.

It has been over two years since her death, but her memory is with me stronger every day. It's hard to wipe out the suffering she went through. But each time I think of that, I also remember how strong she was in Christ.

You know, it was hard for me to pray then. I stood by and watched others pray and wondered how a merciful God could allow this Christian woman to suffer so. It seemed to me those prayers were not answered because she only got weaker. It wasn't long until I knew she wasn't ever going to get well, but she was going to die. That thought was pure torture to me, but as the time passed and I stood by watching her frail body ache all over, it became torture to watch her live. I knew she wanted to be released from her pain. That's when I prayed, "God, please don't let her suffer like this; if she can't get well, please take her with You."

Looking back, I think this was my first real communication with God. When the time came, I could only feel relieved for her. Finally God had taken her to rest, and I was grateful.

Death came. Something I had never really known, and yet I was prepared for it. She was ready. I know she is in heaven. It is now that I cry, not for her, but for myself and my children. How I wish they could have known her. How I wish I had expressed more appreciation for her endless, unselfish sacrifices for me.

It's too late for regrets. I can't go through life hating myself for what I should have done. I can only live for the future. I know if I ever expect to see her again, that future must be living for God. He is the only one who really knows. I wish I had known Him better sooner.

Mother knew Him. He was her closest friend. He was her greatest comforter. She never could have stood what she did without Him. Now, I have a pain. Not like hers, but the pain of a broken heart. I know through prayer He will also comfort me.

Remember how Mother held out her hand to you and you would pray for her? Well, I have never asked for anyone to pray for me, but I am now. Dr. Nelson, I am asking you to pray for me, and I believe only prayer can help. Thank you and God bless you.

Pat Eatherly

Someone once said that confession is good for the soul. May I shout "Amen!" A flood of tears poured out.

I felt such release. It was good to unlock the hidden parts of my heart. *Why hadn't I done this long ago? Did I read my letter correctly? Had I actually requested prayer for myself? Why was it so hard to admit my personal needs? Yes, perhaps prayer was the key.*

The Bible says in 1 Peter 5:6-7, "Humble yourselves therefore under the mighty hand of God, that he may exalt you in due time: Casting all your care upon him; for he careth for you."

I felt I had humbled myself before God. Dr. Nelson's reply revealed God's love to me in his answer. He wrote:

May 8, 1970

Dear Pat,

Your very thoughtful letter came, and it so well expressed the inevitable anguish and pain we feel when a loved one dies. No matter who the person is or the spiritual resources he has, this pain seems to be almost inevitable.

In your case, the long period of lingering suffering by your mother would add to the pain. Your mother was indeed a great Christian. She had a vital faith in God. She did not question why—as many of us who watched her suffer did. There is much mystery to suffering.

As to the feeling that you didn't express your appreciation to her, no one ever does, I feel. However, you did express it in the most practical way a person could—by ministering to her and sticking by her in the hours when she needed you most. No one could have done more than you did. She was unselfish enough that she didn't ask for more.

Pearls are made from pain. The oyster may have a foreign irritant invade its shell—a piece of sand, etc. It secretes an ointment which seals it off and forms what we call a pearl. The painful experiences of life sealed off by the Holy Spirit are turned into pearls.

May God give you comfort.

Sincerely,

David A. Nelson

What a welcome letter! *You mean God's intent wasn't to punish me?* I'm not sure when this idea crept into my thinking, but it was alive with self-pity nourishing it along. Like a soiled garment, I cast it aside immediately. There were far more productive steps to take and ideas to think about now that the veil of misunderstanding had been lifted.

Maybe, I thought, *if God could heal my guilt about Mother, He could even bring Dad and me back together.*

21

Unexpected House Guest

"God's Word is like a bubble bath," stated Ruth Moore, the enthusiastic teacher for Southcliff's Tuesday-morning Bible study. She vividly illustrated the cleansing power of Christ's message when applied to our lives.

Yes, I thought, *a bubble bath, refreshing and cleansing. That's what I want.* She made it sound so simple.

I recalled the life-style into which Gene and I had fallen. Although we attended church regularly, bad habits had subtly stolen away that clean feeling. We often had the so-called "happy hour" to contend with at business and social affairs. Drinking left me with a twinge of guilt, but I steadily squelched the call of my conscience. I found it easier to rationalize my behavior than to correct it. After all, I didn't want to appear prudish to my husband or his business associates. Drunkenness itself was detestable to me, but I never allowed myself more than one or two social drinks.

Attending Southcliff faithfully opened my eyes to see more clearly what it meant to live a Christian life. I hadn't sufficiently considered how my example was affecting others. Gene and I had made so many friends who had such a good time without liquor as a part of their entertainment—so drinking was becoming less and less a temptation. However, the subject was never actually brought up or discussed.

I was beginning to change, and I wanted Gene to change, too. Many times in Sunday School I would hear the ladies talk about their husbands being the spiritual leaders of their homes. They told about having family devotions and praying together.

This all sounded highly idealistic to me. Although I couldn't quite picture this in our home, I admired it in others.

After some time of attending Sunday School, I was convinced that God wanted me to participate more actively. When Mary Jane asked me to be outreach leader for our class, I eagerly accepted. This meant I would visit members on our roll who were not attending regularly. Much to my dismay, these prospects weren't always excited about receiving me or my message. Then I remembered my attitude a few years earlier. *Funny,* I thought, *I used to be nagged by those Christian do-gooders, and now I am the "nagger!"*

Because of my desire to share my newly awakened faith, I decided the best place to start would be right at home. I turned all my zeal toward "straightening out" Gene. In my naïveté of misdirected methods, I was in for a dreadful disappointment. It required a while to realize that it wasn't my place to straighten out my husband. That was a job only God could do. In the meantime I learned another painful lesson.

Although Gene was going to church with me, there was obviously a "missing ingredient" somewhere. A turning point came in our relationship when Gene called from work one night. "Pat," he explained, "I'll be home late tonight; I'm going out to dinner with some men from the office."

That night when he finally came in, I was crushed because his breath reeked with liquor. "Gene," I asked, trying to disguise my disgust, "Where did you-all go for dinner?" Well, it seemed they'd never quite made it past the bar!

I recoiled in resentment and struck out in anger. "Why do you think you have to impress that group of men by drinking with them? Why can't you be strong enough just to say 'no'? It's late, and I was worried about you."

Gene listened until he'd had enough. Shaking his finger in my face he snarled, "I'll decide for myself where I go and what time I come in; so just get off my back!" Angrily, he stomped out of the room.

The next morning when I'd cooled off and he'd sobered up, I tried to explain my position rationally.

"Look, Gene," I said, "I know I can't rule your life and tell you what to do and where to go, but if you continue like this, you are going to destroy my respect for you. It could ultimately ruin our marriage."

"I don't have time to get into this now," he snapped. "I'm going to be late for work." He gulped down the last sip of coffee, grabbed his briefcase and suit coat, then hurriedly slammed the door.

How could he be so cold and unresponsive? I asked myself. An invisible wall between Gene and me seemed to have formed overnight. Alcohol had helped destroy my relationship with Dad. *Could it happen again with my husband?* The thought frightened me.

I didn't know where to turn. I wrestled with the idea of calling Brother Minton. I desperately wanted some wise Christian counsel. Hesitantly, I called the church office and made an early-afternoon appointment.

Nervously, I explained my situation to Brother Minton. He listened intently before offering this advice.

"Pat, your husband, like many men in the business world, is under a great deal of pressure. He's thrust into a world every day that is filled with people who hate God." He looked directly across the desk into my eyes and asked, "Do you pray for him during the day?"

Before I could answer, he kept talking, "Gene is working hard to make a living to give you and your daughters the things he thinks are important to you."

My mind began spinning with instant replays of our life. I'd always put such a heavy emphasis on having a nice home. Now the atmosphere inside that home was, by far, more important. I wanted Christ's love in every room. Gene was still working for the material items that bring only temporary happiness.

I'd been so worried about revealing this episode to our pastor for fear of his thinking harshly of Gene. But Brother Minton wasn't tearing him down; he was building him up.

He concluded, "Pat, Gene loves you, and I believe he wants to please you."

He does? Tears stung my eyes. *He loves me and needs me?* "Oh, dear God," I silently prayed, "let me run to my husband's arms and tell him, 'I'll never let you down.' "

Brother Minton prayed with me. I left with my spirits lifted. As I drove home, I thought what a poor attempt I'd made to change the man I loved. Christ seemed to be whispering, "Love your husband as he is, and I'll take care of the rest."

That afternoon I busied myself with house cleaning and preparation of the evening meal. I stopped to answer the ringing phone. My heart pounded as I heard Gene's voice. Would he think I had betrayed him if he knew about my visit with the preacher?

"Honey, I've been thinking about what you said." Gene sounded a little shaky. "And you're right. Many times like last night would destroy our marriage." I stood there stunned, not knowing how to answer.

He added, "You mean too much to me to ever let that happen. I want to tell you I'm sorry and that it will never happen again."

"Oh, thank you, Lord! Thank you, thank you, thank you," I breathed in prayer. I sensed God's taking control. His presence was real to me. I could see and feel the changes in my life.

Our church began advertising a revival. Posters were plastered throughout the building announcing the coming of a special evangelist, Brian Willersdorf from Australia. His handsome face smiled from the bulletin boards to announce his coming arrival. Gene and I heard he was an excellent speaker and considered going to hear him.

One ordinary evening after I'd tucked the girls into bed and settled beside Gene to watch TV, we were interrupted by the telephone. Answering, I heard Brother Minton's voice. I caught

Gene's attention to turn down the volume. "It's the preacher," I mouthed.

"Pat," Brother Minton said very casually, "I have a favor to ask of you and Gene."

A favor. From us? My thoughts rushed ahead of our conversation, wondering what it could be.

In his relaxed, cheerful mood, he asked "You know about our evangelist who will be coming to Southcliff, don't you?"

"Yes, I do," I answered, questioning his reason for asking.

"Well, Brian and his wife Christine are a fine young couple. They have a baby girl, also. Did you know that?"

"No, I didn't," I admitted, wondering why he was telling me.

"Joyce and I were planning for them to stay in our home this week while they are in our church, but something awful has happened."

"Really?" I quizzed. "What has happened?"

"Our children have come down with the chicken pox," he explained. We were wondering if you and Gene would allow them to stay in your lovely home."

Our home? A special evangelist in our home? I felt honored but unsure. *Yet, it would be such a privilege. How could I refuse?*

"Of course, Brother Minton," I heard myself offering. We would be glad to have them stay with us."

With mixed emotions, we welcomed Brian and Christine Willersdorf and their daughter, Karen Lea. Formalities soon melted with the good-natured charm of this handsome couple. They captivated us with their easy manners and Australian accents.

Dawn and Paige enjoyed playing with the Willersdorfs' cuddly baby girl. One evening as we were talking, Brian inquired, "Dawn, if you had one wish, what would you wish for?"

Her immediate reply was, "I would wish for a baby sister just like Karen."

"Well," Brian mused, "You know how you get one, don't you?"

I began to squirm. *Don't you think a seven-year-old is a bit too young to learn about the birds and bees?* I thought.

Brian carried on, "Dawn, if you truly want a baby sister, all you have to do is pray for one."

I breathed a sigh of relief.

We grew so fond of the Willersdorf's that we gave a party for them, so others could come to know them better. The party was fun. Interesting people crowded the living room. They were friends from our church. I couldn't help comparing this occasion with other parties in the past. There was an indescribable difference.

Brother Minton came over and spoke to me. "Pat, I just want to express my appreciation again for allowing Brian and Christine to stay with you."

I was so full of gratitude for these new friends, I began to thank him. "Brother Minton," I exulted, "You didn't realize what you were doing by putting them in our home."

A slow smile crossed his face and he replied, "Oh, yes, I did."

I smiled back and continued, "They've meant so much to us. I feel we've grown spiritually during their stay." Then hesitantly I admitted, "But I'm afraid it'll go away."

"No," he assured me. "It will only grow."

Not long after the Willersdorfs went back to Australia, I experienced some irregularities in my monthly cycle. It had been awhile since I'd had a physical checkup, so I made an eleven o'clock appointment with my doctor. I could meet Gene for lunch afterwards.

Driving downtown to Gene's office after my doctor's appointment, I wondered how I would break the news to him. "Mrs. Eatherly," the doctor had stated matter-of-factly, "the only thing I have to report from your checkup is that you are pregnant."

How could this be? I'm thirty-two years old. Both girls are in school, and I sold every stick of baby furniture when we moved here. We'll have to start all over. Then again, it might be fun having a brand-new little one to hold and love. I grew warm with the thought.

Gene was alone when I walked into his office and I was pleased. Somehow I couldn't wipe that big grin off my face. "Gene," I've got some important news for you."

"You do? Well, let's have it."

"I'm pregnant."

"You're what?"

"You heard me right," I confirmed. "We're going to have a baby!"

"Honey," Gene's eyes lit up. "I can't believe it!" He walked over to me, slipped his arm around my waist, and suggested, "Well, let's go to lunch and celebrate."

All through lunch we giggled like a couple of giddy kids. "Do you think we should tell the girls right away or keep it a secret?" I asked Gene.

We decided we weren't good at keeping secrets. That evening we sat down in the den to tell Dawn and Paige.

Gene cleared his throat and began, "Girls, Mother and I are going to be getting something new for our house. Do you know what it is?" Their eyes brightened with curiosity.

"We will be having an addition to our family," he teased.

Dawn jumped up and shouted, "I knew it. I knew it all the time. A baby! I prayed for one."

Gene and I looked at each other dumbfounded. We had forgotten all about that conversation she'd had with Brian. Do you suppose . . . no . . . do you really suppose that's how this happened?

22

Thirst for God

"Mommy, can we go get a Slurpee? I'm so hot," Paige begged. She and Dawn had been jumping on our trampoline while Gene mowed the lawn in the sweltering Texas sun.

"Go ask your daddy." I knew they would have no trouble persuading him.

Brushing the dirt and grass clippings from his cutoffs, Gene loaded me and the girls into the car and drove to our neighborhood convenience store.

"I want a cherry-flavored one," Dawn ordered from the backseat.

"I want a lime one," echoed Paige.

"Come on in the store with me, girls, and you can get whatever you want," Gene invited. "Pat, are you coming in?" he asked.

"Yes, I think I will, it's too hot to sit and wait," I answered. I was eight months pregnant, and it was an effort to get in and out of the car.

While Gene and the girls placed their orders, I glanced around the store. Passing by the glass refrigerated showcase, I decided my appetite didn't crave a sweet, syrupy drink. Instead, I opened the door and reached for a cold beer. That sounded good on this hot August Saturday afternoon. *Surely one wouldn't hurt.* Before taking it to the counter for Gene to pay, I popped open the top and took a big sip.

"Lady! What are you doing?" The cashier shrieked. "Don't you know it's against the law to open beer in the store?" she reprimanded.

No, I didn't. But I was sure I'd never forget. *She certainly is making a big deal of it,* I thought. Gene fumbled hurriedly for his billfold as our order was rung up. I felt people staring at us. Dawn and Paige clutched their giant plastic cups piled high with flavored ice.

"Mommy, want a drink? Mine's the best," Dawn offered. Traces of dirty fingerprints were already visible on the sweating cup.

"No thank you, honey," I resisted effortlessly.

I was only too glad to leave the store after my embarrassing episode.

"Only one more month, and it'll be time for our new baby," I reminded the girls on the way home.

I would be thrilled. This summer had been absolutely miserable.

"Mommy, stay outside and watch us do our new tricks on the trampoline . . . please," the girls urged as we drove into our driveway.

"OK, but just for a little while. Mommy's tired. I'm going inside to prop up my feet and rest for awhile," I explained.

The air-conditioned house felt so comfortable after the brief trampoline exhibition in the broiling sun. Picking up the newspaper, I relaxed in my big easy chair.

As I glanced through the paper, I noticed an article entitled "Fetal Alcohol Syndrome." There was a grotesque illustration of a fetus inside a whiskey bottle. I began to read about research done on babies born to drinking mothers. They had begun noticing serious deficiencies in this group of children. For lack of an official name, these children were labled "FLKs," a term which stood for "funny-looking kids."

How terrible, I thought as I kept on reading. The article stated that children born to women who drink heavily while pregnant may be smaller in weight and length and have smaller heads and deficient brain development.

The list seemed endless. It even mentioned that a child born to a female alcoholic might enter the world with the smell of alcohol on its breath, and it could have alcohol withdrawal symptoms!

What about the woman who drinks moderately? I thought. *Is her child also affected?* The article offered no concrete answers. It ended with this paragraph:

The trouble is that we don't know. All of our alcohol studies are retrospective, but I do think that men and women still in their child-bearing years who care about children have one choice to make.

Don't drink.

How alarming! I had never considered my drinking a problem. I endorsed the "drink-in-moderation" viewpoint. *What was wrong with wine with dinner or champagne at weddings?*

Of course, I had read and also experienced the awful mishaps that can occur when a person is under the influence of alcohol. But now I began to examine the effects of alcohol from a mother's perspective.

Why did I drink anyway?

To quench my thirst? Nonalcoholic beverages could do as well. Because I like the taste? Because it relaxes me? Surely, I could find more creative means of relaxation.

The most important thought to me, as I continued to weigh the good and bad, was my responsibility to our children, both born and unborn.

I folded the paper, leaned my head back, and closed my eyes. The scene at the store a short time ago raced through my mind. Here I was eight months pregnant drinking a beer with my two girls looking up to me. It was repulsive to view my image from this new vantage point. What kind of example was I to my children?

Prayerfully, I considered what God would have me do. Didn't Brother Minton recently preach a sermon about being a stumbling block to others? I picked up my Bible to search for that Scripture. It was 1 Corinthians 8:9: "But take heed lest by any means this liberty of yours become a stumblingblock to them that are weak."

"Dear Heavenly Father," I prayed. "I've been seeking Your will for my life. I even asked You to show me if there was any sin in my life that was keeping me from being all that You wanted me to be. So many times, I must admit there was a tinge of guilt about drinking. Thank you for showing me so vividly that drinking is wrong for me. From now on, Lord, I promise You that I will never drink again."

I felt such release. It was as if a weighty burden was lifted from me. I felt free of another obstacle that was keeping me from being close to Christ. The battle on this issue was over.

My thirst grew more intense for God.

23

"God Made Her"

It was barely daylight. I woke out of a restless night's sleep. Perhaps if I went to the bathroom. I would be relieved of this heavy pressure. Suddenly an uncontrollable warm fluid gushed out.

"Gene!" I called urgently, "I think my water just broke. Call Dr. Shannon."

I headed back to the bedroom and sat on the edge of the bed while my husband dialed. He quickly handed the receiver to me.

I explained my symptoms to the doctor. "Meet me at Harris Hospital as soon as possible," Dr. Shannon ordered.

"What'll we do with Dawn and Paige at this hour of the morning?" Gene asked.

"Call Lyndith," I said. We roused two sleepy girls and led them across the street to our neighbor.

Soon we were driving to the hospital, suitcase in hand, trying hard to stay within the speed limit. Signs of daylight shone in the pinkish, streaked sky.

Dawn and Paige had been born within two hours after entering the hospital. They were both normal deliveries. I knew this baby was going to be even faster, especially since my water had broken at home.

"Are you OK, Hon?" Gene questioned, pulling into the hospital emergency entrance.

"Yes, I'm fine," I assured him, trying to be brave. My labor pains had begun.

The automatic doors opened wide as we entered Harris Hospital. Before we spoke a word, the admission clerk signaled for a wheelchair. My condition needed no explanation. I was whisked off to the obstetrics floor, Gene trailing behind.

Dr. Shannon soon appeared and ordered a mild sedative to relax me before time to begin the caudal block. He had explained that the medication would be given intravenously to make me comfortable but not put me out. I wanted to be awake to watch the birth.

After I was prepped and probed, Dr. Shannon allowed Gene to enter the labor room. The pain came hard, then gradually slackened, then went away. After twelve exhausting hours of this repeating pattern, I was wheeled into the delivery room. I tried to see in the mirror that had been carefully adjusted.

Suddenly Dr. Shannon announced to the nurse to prepare for a Caesarean section.

Hastily, I was lifted onto a stretcher and moved to the operating room. My head was foggy. The glare of bright lights penetrated my heavy eyelids. The next thing I remembered was a mask covering my face and someone ordering, "Take a deep breath . . . as deep as you can."

I did. I would have done anything to be relieved of this misery. Before the gas had time to take effect I felt the pressure of an incision being made through my skin. Fortunately the area was partially numb from novocaine administered for the usual episiotomy.

I was transferred from the operating room to recovery. I looked up and slowly focused on Gene. He leaned over and gently took my hand.

"Oh, Gene," I whispered, "It was a nightmare." I could still feel the sensation of the knife before I had been completely sedated. Traces of tears were on my cheeks.

"It's going to be all right," Gene comforted me. "We have another baby girl."

"She's a pretty little thing, too." I turned my head to recognize Albert White, Mary Jane's husband standing on the other side of me. I learned later that he had spent the entire afternoon in the waiting room with Gene.

"Would you like to see her?" the nurse asked, rolling my bed to the glass window. I nodded, too weak to answer.

The nurse on the other side of the nursery waited to assist. Albert took the pink identification card saying, "Girl Eatherly," and held it up to the window. When the baby was held for viewing, Albert grinned so big the nurse thought it was his baby. Gene tried to correct her in sign language, "No, it's mine!"

I couldn't restrain a chuckle watching these two tired men enjoying their childish shenanigans.

The next day I entered the information in the artistically arranged pages of my new baby book.

NAME	Tricia Beth Eatherly
DATE OF BIRTH	September 29, 1971
TIME	6:02 P.M.
WEIGHT	6 pounds 10 1/2 ounces
LENGTH	20 1/2 inches

My room soon filled with flowers and friends. It had been so different with our first child, Dawn, who was born after we had lived in Tucson for only one month. I had known no one. Of course, there had been a few more friends to congratulate Paige's arrival fifteen months later, but nothing like now. I was overwhelmed with the expressions of Christian love shown in so many practical ways. Georgia Ann Scott, a friend from church, cared for the girls the whole time I was in the hospital.

Every day I received beautiful cards that I enjoyed reading over and over again. A poignantly expressed letter from my mother-in-law in California awakened a part of me that I thought was a well-guarded secret. She wrote:

> To our newest little angel, Tricia Beth. We are so proud
> to have another rosebud added to our family tree. I am
> longing to see and hold you in my arms. You will share

a place in my heart with two precious sisters. God bless
and guide you, Tricia, all your life.

Then she ended with a statement that touched a tender spot
in my heart:

You will have a guardian angel named Mary watching
over you.
Love from two very proud grandparents.

The realization that this new baby would never know my
mother was bittersweet. I vowed that I would teach Tricia to
love her grandmother, even though she was in heaven. I wondered if Tricia would have a guardian angel named Mary to
watch over her. The thought gave me a sense of Mother's
presence and admonished me to raise her grandchild to know
and love God. My heart pounded to control the emotions well-
ing up inside me. *I must not feel sad,* I thought. *Mother wouldn't
want that.* Funny, how I sensed an unseen touch of guidance,
even though she was no longer with me physically. My love for
her deepened with each experience of life. Even the pain preced-
ing this birth helped me to identify with how she must have
suffered for over two years before her death. I felt ashamed to
complain; my pain seemed so small in comparison.

Of course Dad didn't acknowledge Tricia's arrival. But after
two previous unacknowledged births, I didn't expect it.

Gradually my strength returned. With each visit Gene
helped me exercise as we slowly walked down the hall. "Dawn
and Paige can't wait for you to bring their new sister home,"
he said.

"It's only two more days," I reminded him. I'd been marking
the time on my calendar.

The time passed quickly, and the day arrived to wrap Tricia
in her softest pink blanket and take her home. The nurse had
trouble arranging all the flowers and personal belongings on the
cart as we set out to the car. Gene helped, with obvious nervous

excitement. Finally, I was seated in the car with our precious possession in my arms.

Gene could hardly keep his eyes on the street for glancing at Tricia sleeping peacefully. The sun felt warm and I felt content. As we turned onto Wrigley Way, our home was a welcome sight. How could two weeks have seemed so long?

We walked into a spotlessly clean house. I knew Gene and the girls had prepared carefully for this occasion.

"Now you can put Tricia in her own bed, and let her sleep while we have a bite of lunch," Gene said.

As we sat down to a big bowl of homemade stew a friend had furnished, Gene held my hand and voiced a prayer of thanksgiving that sent tears rolling down my cheeks. God truly sent this baby to us. She was His gift, as all children are.

When three o'clock rolled around, Dawn came tearing into the house from school. She was breathless from racing Paige home to be first to hold her new sister.

Paige wasn't far behind. "My turn, Dawn," she insisted, looking to me for approval. As they took turns cradling Tricia, Gene proudly boasted, "Girls, just look what Mommy and I made."

"Oh, no," Paige replied, shaking her head no. "Dawn prayed for her, God made her, and Mommy had her!"

Dawn was silent for a moment, but not to be outdone, she added, "But Daddy paid for her!"

We all laughed. "Lord, keep this happy moment alive in my heart," I prayed silently. "Thank you for the love that so beautifully binds us together today."

Another of these treasured memories came when Dawn was only nine years old and made her decision to accept Jesus as Lord and Savior. Brother Minton made an appointment to come by our home and talk with her before she was baptized.

After dinner, I bathed Tricia and put her to bed. Dawn and Paige efficiently cleared away the dishes to prepare our home for the preacher's visit. They had become very helpful since

Tricia's birth. Soon there was an expected knock on the door. Brother Minton's athletic build filled the doorway.

"Hello, young ladies," boomed our pastor's cheerful voice. "Where's your baby sister tonight?"

"In bed," Dawn sighed with relief. Some of the new had worn off.

As we were seated in the living room, Brother Minton said, "Dawn, I understand you have just made one of the most important decisions in your life." Then he started explaining the depths of salvation in childlike terms. He pulled a big colorful glove from his suit pocket. "Dawn, do you know what this is?"

Dawn shook her head to indicate "no." Her eyes were glued to the funny-looking glove with each finger a different color.

"This," Brother Minton explained, "is called a 'Good News Glove.' Do you know why?"

Dawn shook her head again. Her eyes still fixed on the glove.

"It's called the 'Good News Glove' because it tells the good news of how you can be a child of God. Now that is good news, isn't it?"

Dawn shook her head in a "yes."

As the preacher placed his large hand into the glove, the fingers clearly displayed words to read. "The 'Good News Glove' tells you four things, Dawn," he explained.

1. God loves me.
2. I have sinned.
3. Jesus died and came alive for me.
4. When I receive Him, I am forgiven and have life forever.

She read each one with him as he explained the colors' significance. The yellow represented God's light. The black was to remind us of sinful darkness. Red told of Christ's shed blood. White was the promise of purity and cleansing.

Brother Minton tenderly asked, "Dawn, have you prayed and asked Jesus into your heart?"

Still speechless, she again nodded in the affirmative.

"Dawn, will you pray with me now as we thank God for your decision?" With our heads bowed, Brother Minton led us in a beautiful prayer of thanksgiving.

"Now Dawn, you see the thumb of the Good News Glove is green. Green represents growth. God wants to teach you how to grow spiritually. Brother Minton turned the glove to the other side which was bright green. Each finger had a key word printed on it. As he wiggled his finger, Dawn read the words, *grow, pray, Bible, obey,* and *tell.*

"That, Dawn, is how we grow spiritually. God wants you to talk with Him in prayer; to learn His words by reading the Bible; to obey what His Word says and to tell this Good News to others."

He removed the glove from his hand and gently placed it on hers. "Now, this is yours to keep to remind you of these things."

"Thank you," Dawn spoke in a whisper. Then she questioned, "Will I be baptized next Sunday?"

"Yes, you certainly will. Your baptism will identify you with other Christians. You know Jesus was baptized, and He wants you to follow His example.

"Brother Minton," I interrupted, "she seems so young to understand all this." Then hesitantly I recalled my own childhood experience. "I was only ten years old when I received Christ and was baptized. Then I strayed away from God's teachings a long time before I came back." With a chuckle to cover up my embarrassment, I confessed, "Perhaps I was too young for it to 'take.' "

"Pat," Brother Minton's eyes bore into mine, "a tender new plant can't grow if you put it into a dark closet. The seed needs light, water, and nourishment. It could be you weren't in a suitable environment for growth."

I thought about what he'd just said and recalled how I was

encouraged to attend church when I lived in Kentucky, but in California, Sundays had no special meaning.

"Dear God," I prayed, "please help me always to create the kind of environment where my children can grow spiritually."

I smiled and thanked our kind pastor as Gene and I walked him to the door. Little did he know how his statement had pruned away a part of my own self-doubts.

Before he left, he shook hands with Dawn, then reached for Paige's hand. As Paige slipped her small hand in his, she looked up to him, stood tall, and with deliberate courage, said, "Brother Minton, when I get older and understand more, I want to be a Christian, too." (Only a few years later, Paige also prayed to receive Christ.)

A magnetic sense of God's love tugged at my heart. God was again at work in our immediate family. I wondered if it were possible that He could even work in my Dad's life.

24

Search for Forgiveness

"Haven't you ever felt like you wanted to forgive your father?" Gene's question haunted me.

Of course, I wanted to forgive him—if he'd only ask! It became obvious that was never going to happen. It was up to me. I'll never forget the day I called him at his new home in Nashville.

By phone Dad sounded as charming and loving as a father could be. We seemed to have a constant stage presence when speaking to each other. Dad told me how busy he'd been writing for the "Johnny Cash Show." There was a special segment called, "Come Along and Ride This Train" which was his responsibility. It was good to hear his voice after *six years;* and although we avoided talking about anything serious, at least the lines of communication were open again.

That summer when our family visited relatives in Kentucky and Tennessee, we drove out to see Dad and Bettie at their home near Nashville on Old Hickory Lake.

Dad showed us around his house. His favorite room was the den which doubled as a recording studio. Through the wooded backyard was a breathtaking view of the lake.

While we nibbled on a plate of fruit and cheese which Bettie had prepared, I handed Dad a book by Dale Evans Rogers called *Woman at the Well.*

"Dad, I thought you'd enjoy this book about your friends, Dale and Roy Rogers."

He smiled approvingly, then laughed, and remarked, "You mean about Frances Smith."

"Frances Smith?" I questioned. Then, I caught on and joined his joke. Frances Smith was Dale Evans's real name before she entered the movies.

We spent several hours together, straining to relax and be natural. Nothing unpleasant was mentioned to mar our pretended normality. We hugged and kissed good-bye as Dad and Bettie promised to stop by to see us the next time they were in Texas. I didn't get my hopes up.

Three years had passed since they'd made that promise, but Dad and Bettie were coming today. They were actually coming to our house in Fort Worth. I was so excited when I received their call, I thought of little else.

As I left to carry two year-old Tricia to the nursery, I examined the house again. Fresh towels were hung in the bathrooms, the windows were sparkling, and the furniture smelled of lemon oil polish. The aroma blended with a smoked brisket baking in the oven. My friend Claire Farris would bring Tricia home from nursery school, freeing me to handle any last-minute details.

The exact hour of their arrival was unknown, and I began to worry that although I had supper planned that they might be hungry for lunch. Hastily, I jumped in the car to drive to the nearest convenience store to buy sandwich fixings. Minutes later while entering our driveway, I viewed our home with pride. Gene even had the yard manicured. All was in order.

As I walked to the door, I noticed a note squeezed between a small opening. *Someone must have stopped by while I was gone,* I thought. I opened the note to read: "Sorry, we missed you. Dad."

Unbelieving, I reexamined each word. "Sorry, we missed you. Dad." Every muscle in my body became tense. I shook my head as if this mistake would go away. *This can't be. I've waited all my married life for my father to come visit, and he couldn't wait five minutes!* Hurt turned to overpowering anger.

Maybe if I hurry I could catch up with him! I jumped back into my car and screeched out of the driveway. Speeding through the neighborhood, I took the first ramp onto Loop 820. My reasoning mind finally overtook my emotions, realizing this was an impossible chase. I had no idea where Dad had gone. I slowly turned back toward home.

He just died, I thought revengefully. My vision blurred with tears. "I'm sorry, Dad," I confessed out loud, "as far as I'm concerned, you just died. I'll never leave myself open for you to hurt me again."

When I arrived home, Claire was waiting for me with Tricia. "What's wrong?" she questioned.

She compassionately tried to console me before she left. My heart was heavy as I carried Tricia into our carefully prepared home. I looked around, and tears gushed from my eyes again. After busying Tricia with her toys, I went to the phone to dial Gene. Before it rang, I hung up. I decided to call our good friend Billie Hanks first. He is an evangelist and a genuine man of God. *Maybe he'll have some answers.*

Billie listened attentively as I explained what had happened. "Pat, let's have a word of prayer right now about this," he suggested.

I bowed my head as Billie prayed over the phone, ". . . and Lord, we want to thank you for what happened today, knowing that in your timing, all things work together for good. In Jesus' Name, Amen."

"Thank you, Billie," I forced myself to answer politely and hung up. *He just doesn't understand,* I thought. *No one understands.*

Even Gene was filled with idealistic nonsense. His advice didn't set well either.

"Pat," he reminded me, "if you're going to love your father at all, you're going to have to do it with *agape* love."

We'd been studying about the word *agape* at church. It means Christlike love. Loving unconditionally, never expecting anything in return. That's how God loves us, we were taught. Well, all I wanted was to be loved in return. Was that asking too much?

Oblivious to the fact that this incident had caused any turmoil, Dad called several months later, again announcing that he would be coming through Fort Worth. This time I prepared myself to shield off any disappointment. But, just in case he did make it, I bought him a very special gift. In all the years of seeing the name "Merle Travis" in print, I'd never seen it on a Bible. I carefully selected a red leather copy of *The Living Bible* and had "Merle Travis" printed in gold. When he came, it would be lying casually on the coffee table in the den.

And came he did! Dad visited our home for the first time. That evening we somehow found ourselves chatting in our den just like any ordinary family might do. As the conversation wore thin, Tricia toddled over to the coffee table, picked up the red leather-bound book, and announced, "Grandpa, here's your Bible."

My eyes followed every move as my heart recorded this miraculous event. Dad picked up Tricia and sat her on his lap, looked down at the Bible, and said, "Why, it's got my name on it!"

"Yes, Dad," I answered. "Open it and read Psalm 139." I quickly helped him find Psalms. "It's a modern version, without the thee's and thou's."

He began reading, and I realized it was the first time in my life I'd ever heard my father read from the Bible. Furthermore, he had my baby daughter in his lap. *Maybe we could finally have a normal family relationship,* I dared to think. What a glorious sight. I remembered Billie's prayer. But this long-awaited scene faded away too quickly.

Years went by with little or no contact between Dad and our family. Dawn and Paige grew into teenagers. The busy days numbed the hurt since there was little time to dwell on the past. There were always cookies to bake or carpools to drive or a new dress to make. I simply put thoughts of my father behind me. At least I tried.

Unofficial rumors led me to learn that the marriage between Dad and Bettie had ended. He was now in the company of a longtime friend, Dorothy Thompson. I was told she'd accompanied him on October 10, 1977, when he was inducted into the Country Music Hall of Fame. I'd learned he was now living in Tahlequah, Oklahoma.

He had once again become a stranger to us. Then, unexpectedly one cold December evening, he called.

"Patty, this here's your ol' Pappy." It wasn't hard to guess Dad had been drinking. After a confusing time of trying to make sense out of his conversation, he spoke these poetic and philosophical words. His thick speech slurred:

> Know me as I am,
> Love me if you will,
> Hate me if you must.

What did he mean by this? Was he asking me if I hated him? "Dad," I answered his unspoken question, "I don't hate you. There have been times when I've been disappointed. There have been lots of times when I didn't understand, but I don't hate you."

His conversation continued, and he began making ugly accusations about Mother. It had been over ten years since her death. *Why,* I wondered, *after all these years would he want to pick on her and tear her down? She had never spoken unkindly of him. He must've been feeling extra low to stoop to such extremes.* He'd avoided speaking of her through the years. Now, all of a sudden, he unfairly badgered her memory. When we finally hung up I tried to rationalize that once again alcohol was speaking and not Merle Travis.

I answered his accusations with this letter.

February 7, 1978

Dear Dad,

I know my mother did some things that were wrong. But so have you and I. God has forgiven her, and so have I. His power of forgiveness has reached me, and it could reach you, if you would let it.

First John 1:9 says, "If we confess our sins, he is faithful and just to forgive us our sins, and to cleanse us from all unrighteousness."

There is nothing I would like more than to see you choose God's way. If you do, we would have a whole eternity to make up for whatever we might have missed here.

Think about it. I'll be praying for you.

Your daughter,

Pat

25

Emotional Blindness

Sunday mornings were usually a rush, "coaching" three daughters to dress and arrive at church on time. However, this Sunday was one of those unusual mornings when we were not only on time, but were actually early. Slipping comfortably into our regular pew, we felt at home.

I glanced around and caught the eye of Mr. and Mrs. Pete Riels who were long-time members of our congregation. Pete and his wife, Helen, were devoted country music fans and often spoke to me of their admiration for my father. I tried to hide my embarrassment when they seemed to know more about his latest accomplishments than I did. But, this morning, my embarrassment could not be hidden.

"Pat," Pete reported, grinning with obviously happy news, "I saw your picture on the cover of your father's album." Helen, immaculately dressed in her favorite shade of purple, smiled over his shoulder.

"My picture?" I questioned suspiciously. I laughed and jokingly asked, "Was it a monkey?" thinking they must be kidding.

"No," Pete answered emphatically. "It's you. You're standing in front of a big historical marker which was dedicated to Merle in Ebenezer, Kentucky. The album is called, "Merle Travis, the Guitar Player." He added, "I can get you a copy if you don't already have one."

Before I could answer, Pete had read my expression and promised to bring me an album next Sunday. "As a matter of fact," he invited, "Why don't you and Gene go with us to the

Johnnie High Country Music Revue this Saturday? They have great country musicians."

The church organ reminded us it was time to end our conversation. Gene and I couldn't refuse their enthusiastic invitation.

That next Saturday night we found ourselves at Will Rogers Auditorium for the show. The star for the night was Hank Thompson. Ironically he was the ex-husband of Dorothy, now Dad's new wife. After a flamboyant introduction, Hank entered the spotlight to a cheering crowd. He dazzled his fans with songs that began to jog my memory, such as "Oklahoma Hills," "Whoa Sailor," and "The Wild Side of Life." Then, much to my surprise, he mentioned Merle Travis and began playing "I'll See You in My Dreams" in that undeniable Travis style.

Quick as a flash he made a joke that was as sad as it was funny: "Yes, folks, I must tell you, Merle's one of my favorite guitar pickers. As a matter of fact, my ol' buddy Trav' is married to my ex-wife."

I could feel the anticipation for the next line from the crowd. Hank's timing was precise when he shook his head quizzically and added, "I reckon that makes us husbands-in-law!" The audience roared with laughter.

I couldn't keep from laughing, too, but deep inside it gave me a sick feeling. Why do show people think they live by a whole different code of morals from everyone else? What makes them any different just because they perform for a living? Does that exempt them from being responsible to their families? Are fans so gullible that they can't see through the phony glamour?

I was glad the Riels couldn't read my thoughts when I thanked them for a wonderful evening.

"Makes you think of your dad again, doesn't it?" Gene probed, studying my mood.

"Yeah," I admitted reluctantly. "I wish things could be different." I began to scheme. "You know what, Gene?"

"No, what, Pat?" Gene exaggerated his response playfully.

"I'm going to call and invite Dad and Dorothy to come have Thanksgiving dinner with us."

Why did such a simple suggestion sound so preposterous? "Yep, that's what I'm going to do," I repeated, convincing myself.

I had learned that Dorothy often visited her parents in Waco, Texas, only eighty miles from us. I gathered my courage and called Dad in Tahlequah, Oklahoma.

As usual, we made pleasant small talk for awhile. Then I asked, "Dad, how about you and Dorothy spending Thanksgiving with us?"

I really didn't expect a "yes," but I still wanted to ask. As I prepared myself for a "no," he kind of hesitated and then thought out loud, "Well, maybe we could do that. Dorothy's sister lives in Fort Worth, and we talked about visiting her."

"Really?" I responded, amazed he was considering it. Then knowing the preparation that Thanksgiving dinner requires, I wanted to know for sure. "Dad, I'll need to go shopping for dinner, and you know how women are planning for company," I chuckled, wondering if he'd ever given such matters any thought. I continued, "I'll need to know soon for sure."

"Well, Patty," his voice pulled back. "I don't know if we could stay and eat with you. It might hurt Dorothy's sister's feelings."

Hurt Dorothy's sister's feelings? Hurt Dorothy's sister's feelings! What about my feelings? Do my ears deceive me? Am I hearing right? Is he actually putting this stranger ahead of me? I'd had enough.

Calmly at first, I said, "Dad, I can't believe what you just said. You seem to have a priority list, and it's not that I'm on the bottom. I'm not even on it!"

"Now, Patty," he raised his voice. "You know my family has always come first."

Talk about a sick joke . . . I laughed right out loud. "Dad, how can you say that? You have three granddaughters, and you hardly even know them . . . and you say your family comes first?"

"Well, that's not the way I want it to be," he answered pitifully.

"Let me say this before I go," I concluded. "I'm tired of trying with you. I just quit. Dad, if we ever get together again, it will have to be up to you." And I meant it!

Even though I imagined that I hid my "father frustrations" from my girls, I was only fooling myself. One hot summer afternoon, while our family was having fun at a neighborhood swim club, nine-year-old Tricia surprised me with a question about my lingering upset over Dad. "Mommy," she asked innocently, "will we ever get to see your daddy again?"

"Your daddy," she called her own grandfather. I thought about her question for a moment. Dad and I hadn't spoken in two years.

Sadly, I answered, "Tricia, I don't know. Would you like to?"

"Uh huh," she nodded.

"Then why don't you write him and tell him so," I suggested.

She did, and to my absolute astonishment she received an immediate reply in large artist's print, complete with a fancy cartoon illustration. Dad's letter read:

> July 18, 1980
> Dear Tricia:
>
> How wonderful it was to get your letter! It sounds like you're quite an athlete. You swim on the Fort Worth Swim Team and water-ski! Now I can go around telling people that my granddaughter, Tricia, is an award-winning swimmer! That makes me very happy for you, and proud for me.
>
> My wife, Dorothy, and I live about 14 miles from an Oklahoma town named Tahlequah. (Towel-e-quaw) It's

the capital of the Cherokee Nation, so there's lots of Indian people here. Their skin is a nice brown color, so they don't have to get out in the sun to get a tan.

We live on Lake Tenkiller. As I'm writing to you, I can look out at the lake and trees and see no houses at all. We live at the end of the road, so there's no cars passing by. It's nice to get up in the morning with the birds singing, then to hear the whippoorwills at night.

Let me say once more how very happy I was to receive your letter.

I'm sure we'll get to come and see you one of these days. I'd like that very much.

Tell your family that I said "Hello," and never forget that I love you.

Your Grandpa—

Merle Travis

Shortly after sending Tricia the letter, Dad began mailing her many record albums, such as, "The Merle Travis Story," "Light Singin' & Heavy Pickin' Merle Travis," and "Country Guitar Giants, Merle Travis & Joe Maphis." Each was personally autographed with,

To My Granddaughter, Tricia.

Love, Grandpa

Merle Travis

Tricia's excitement usually ended shortly after the wrappings were torn away, but I carefully read every word on the jacket covers.

One paragraph particularly intrigued me. It was the story written by Dad for the Merle Travis and Joe Maphis album. I read:

When Joe and I were young fellers, one of the places to go
to flirt with girls was at church. Not the big, red brick churches
where everybody dressed up and the choir sang slow, mournful
songs that bounced back from stained-glass windows. Not at
all! We went to small, white weatherboarded churches that got
their light from coal-oil (kerosene) lamps. Everybody in the
church sang, hands were clapped in tempo, and feet kept time
patting on the floor. The songs were fast and spirited. The
churches were places preachers delivered their sermons for the
glory of God and not for money. They were Holiness or Pen-
tecostal churches. A lot of folks looked down on them and
called them "holy-rollers."

At the age of nineteen, I married a girl whose father was a
Holiness preacher. He worked in the mines for money and
preached to save souls.

Hank Williams wrote a song during his short stay on earth
that sounds exactly like one of the old Holiness hand-clapping,
foot-patting, shouting songs. We played it; it's titled, "I Saw the
Light."

When I was alone I listened to the skillful arrangements and
lyrics on these records. I began to feel homesick for my father.
What had I done to turn him against me? Why when he mailed
these albums, couldn't he even write my name? Was he using
Tricia to express what he couldn't say to me?

Many times in searching for answers in my life, I recalled
books that I'd read. Recently I'd read *What Wives Wish Their
Husbands Know About Women* by Dr. James Dobson. I remembered a letter Dr. Dobson had written to a woman he called
Martha. She had experienced similar emotions with her father
when he declined her invitation to her son's wedding. If Dr.
Dobson's advice helped her, maybe it would help me. I pulled
the book off my shelf and read.

Martha, I am more convinced every day that a great portion

of our adult effort is invested in the quest for that which was unreachable in childhood. The more painful the early void, the more we are motivated to fill it later in life. Your dad never met the needs that a father should satisfy in his little girl, and I think you are still hoping he will miraculously become what he has never been. Therefore, he constantly disappoints you—hurts you—rejects you. I think you will be less vulnerable to pain when you accept the fact that he cannot, nor will he ever, provide the love and empathy and interest that he should. It is not easy to insulate yourself in this way. I'm still working to plug a few vacuums from my own tender years. But it hurts less to expect nothing than to hope in vain.

I would guess that your dad's own childhood experiences account for his emotional peculiarities, and can perhaps be viewed as his own unique handicap. If he were blind, you would love him despite his lack of vision. In a sense, he is emotionally "blind." He is unable to see your needs. He is unaware of the hurt behind the unpleasant incidents and disagreements . . . His handicap makes it impossible for him to perceive your feelings and anticipation. If you can accept your father as a man with a permanent handicap—one which was probably caused when he was vulnerable—you will shield yourself from the ice pick of rejection . . .[5]

That letter could have been written to me personally. I wanted to apply Dr. Dobson's wisdom to my situation. Thoughtfully, I sat down at my desk and wrote Dad a letter asking him to forgive me if there was anything I'd done that kept him from expressing his love to me.

On October 29, 1980, I received this reply:

Dear Pat:

As the poet wrote;
"At last the toil-encumbered days are over The airs of noon are mellow as the morn . . ."

Yes, it's autumn again, but the airs of noon yesterday were not so mellow. They were downright cold. Still, I felt a bit of warmth in finding your letter among the other mail that had collected in the two weeks we've been away.

I'm sure you want a truthful answer to your first few lines which said in part, "If there is anything I've done that keeps you from expressing your love to me, I ask your forgiveness."

As for forgiving you, that's automatic. How could I say such a thing as, "No, you're not forgiven"? But then, how could things like this happen?

Year before last you called a few days before Thanksgiving. You were as charming as ever on the phone, and I was thinking to myself what a grand gal my first-born daughter is. Then you politely told me you wanted me to come and have Thanksgiving dinner with you and your family. We had made plans to go to Waco and have dinner with Dorothy's aged parents, but perhaps we could run up to Fort Worth a little later. As I hope you remember, you didn't buy that sort of thing at all.

Once again you took it upon yourself to verbally lay me flat. Your voice trembled as a barrage of dramatic abuses belittled me from every possible angle. I was accused of thinking only of myself, thinking more of other people than of my own flesh and blood. When I sneaked one phrase in somehow, explaining that I liked to think my family came first, you said with a sarcastic quaver, "Ha! that's a laugh!" In some sort of ironic way it was nice to think there was a little humor in a reprobatic jerk such as I.

One thing you brought up in your wrathful oratory. The regretful fact that I have three young ladies who are my grandchildren, still I hardly know them. That's not at all the way I'd like things to be. Not at all!

Pat, you must believe I have feelings too. I also have a memory of sort.

Try to think how I felt the morning when Gene and you

were leaving the little guest house on Ranchito. I was sicker than you'd believe. That's why I was sitting on the ground leaning back against the warm building when I whined something like, "I wish you two didn't have to leave . . ." I looked up at a very pretty face that scowled down with scorn at the only father she'll ever have. From her came a scorching lecture. I was told how no good I was, how shiftless, self-centered and obnoxious a person I'd continued to be.

I have no idea where you came up with the idea that you could blaze away at me time and time again. Is it because I didn't spend time by your poor suffering mother's bedside, because you sincerely believe I'm so far below your standards that I can be taken to task any time you choose? Could it be because you've been semi-pampered just about all your life, or is it because you're a lot like your father?

Now to repeat . . . Thanksgiving is not far away. That's the day two years ago when Dorothy and I stayed right here at home. I had no desire to go to Waco and have dinner with her parents. They're old now and have obtained some wisdom along the way, I suppose. They never called for the purpose of bawling me out.

But I love the one who did,

Your Dad,

Merle Travis

The ice pick of rejection was positioned to penetrate as I read Dad's letter. But somehow this time I was protected. A shield of new understanding allowed me to guard my own hurt long enough to see through the eyes of a man who was emotionally blind. Even though this letter opened old wounds, at least Dad wrote what was on his mind. Perhaps the exposure of seeing beyond the superficial could open a bit of honest communication.

NOTE

5. James Dobson, *What Wives Wish Their Husbands Knew About Women* (Wheaton, IL: Tyndale House, 1977), p. 181.

26

"Feudin' Over"

Why, I asked myself, *do you put so much importance on having a father-daughter relationship? You are a forty-two-year-old woman with a husband who loves you. You are a mother of three daughters who depend on you. Why can't you release this fantasy of having an ideal, loving father?*

Sometimes on those rare occasions when I found myself at home alone, I'd listen to Dad's records simply to hear his voice. Then to appease the child in me, I'd sneak out the bulging scrapbooks and relive the magical days when I'd been proud to be called "Merle's girl." While flipping through the pages of my past, my memory smiled at the picture of the little girl in finger curls. There I was with my father's hand on my shoulder as I held the prized possession Dad had been given—the key to the city of Drakesboro, Kentucky.

As a little girl, I'd secretly yearned for that big, shiny gold key, but I didn't dare ask for it. It belonged to entertainer Merle Travis, who was being welcomed back to Drakesboro to celebrate his first hit song, "Smoke, Smoke, Smoke (That Cigarette)."

So much had happened since then, I thought. That picture was taken in the late 1940s, and now it was 1981. The past was gone forever. It couldn't be undone or redone. Regardless of what had happened then, I was now responsible for my future. Didn't the Bible speak about that in 1 Corinthians 13:11-13? I took the Bible from my shelf and read:

> . . . when I was a child I spoke and thought and reasoned

as a child does. But when I became a man [a woman] my thoughts grew far beyond those of my childhood, and now I have put away the childish things. In the same way, we can see and understand only a little about God now, as if we were peering at his reflection in a poor mirror; but someday we are going to see him in his completeness, face to face. Now all that I know is hazy and blurred, but then I will see everything clearly, just as clearly as God sees into my heart right now.

There are three things that remain—faith, hope, and love—and the greatest of these is love (TLB).

I picked up a pencil and notebook and wrote a prayer.

Lord Jesus, only you know the struggle in my heart about my attitude toward my earthly father. As best I know how, I have forgiven him. I do love him. I do not pray for a change in him for any selfish motive. I have given to you my long ago desire to have him in the relationship of a father to me and a grandfather to my children. My prayer now is for him as a person—a human being in need of salvation. In need of You.

Is it wrong to accept the facts that have been lived out before me? In no means do I come in an attitude of defeat or self-pity, but in reality. I want to accept the truth . . . whatever that is.

I will continue looking to You in my search for truth. My Christian witness to my dad has turned sour. He doesn't understand.

Then I read in 1 Corinthians 2:14: "But the natural man receiveth not the things of the Spirit of God; for they are foolishness unto him: neither can he know them, because they are spiritually discerned."

So, how can I expect Dad to understand? My witness to him boomeranged with his hurtful question of, "Do you sincerely believe I'm so far below your standards that I can be taken to task any time you choose?"

This hit like a stinging slap in the face, especially after

a letter pouring out my heart and asking for forgiveness for anything that might be keeping him from expressing his love to me.

Strange I should find in your Word in Luke 21:16, "And ye shall be betrayed both by parents, and brethren and kinsfolks, and friends."

Could this be your answer to me? Psalm 27:10 tells me: "When my father and my mother forsake me, then the Lord will take me up."

I know, dear Heavenly Father, that you do have an answer for me. I want to be open in my spirit when it comes.

Until then I rest in your peace, the peace of God which passes all understanding.

Amen.

With my Bible still in my lap, I turned to Matthew 5 and read in verses 44-45: ". . . bless them that curse you, do good to them that hate you, and pray for them which despitefully use you, and persecute you; That ye may be the children of your Father which is in heaven."

Again, I repeated the powerful words I'd just read, "That ye [that's me, Pat Eatherly] may be the children [or child] of your [my] Father which is in heaven."

That's my answer, I realized. *God is my* real *Father. He is the One who sees into my heart. It is He, who has promised "I will never leave thee, nor forsake thee"* (Heb. 13:5).

Gradually, in the following weeks, the love of my "Father" soothed and filled the gnawing emptiness inside me. When I thought about Dad, I could do it with a new inward peace and certainty that my Heavenly Father was in control.

Then on February 21, 1982, it happened. Dad came to visit in our Fort Worth home. I recorded the date in my Bible with the notation, "A long overdue visit with my *earthly* father." Later I learned that he too recorded this date on his calendar with the notation beside it: "Feudin' Over!"

It started with a phone call on Valentine's Day. During the course of the conversation Dad proposed, "Pat, let's forget yesterday and start a new tomorrow." He eagerly accepted our invitation to visit this time.

I'll always remember that late afternoon when my family watched the big black Lincoln Continental pull into our driveway. Dorothy was behind the wheel, and she quickly made her way around the car to help Dad gather his pipe, glasses, and other paraphernalia. I smiled to myself as I caught a glimpse of the clothes, guitars, and record albums filling the backseat. The slowness of Dad's movements and a few added wrinkles reminded me of the time that had passed.

"Hi there, Pat, how 'bout a big hug for your ol' Pappy?" When our arms wrapped around each other, I was grateful for this "New Tomorrow."

Then he turned his attention to his granddaughters. During the last twenty years I'd focused my attention on being a mother to three daughters. Dad hardly knew them. The girls were nineteen, seventeen, and ten years old.

Tricia, our youngest, was taking violin lessons in school. She could play one little ditty that sounded kind of country. She placed a chair on the wide fireplace hearth, turned on an overhead spotlight, and stole her grandfather's heart when she announced, "Grandpa, your stage is ready."

Dad's eyes lit up when he saw Tricia taking her violin out of the case. "I want to play with you," she announced.

"Dorothy," Dad asked his wife, "would you get my Baby Martin out of the car?" Soon Dad and Tricia were playing away to the tune of "Bile Them Cabbage Down." Tricia giggled as Dad sang the lyrics:

> If I had a scoldin' wife,
> I'd whoop her sure as I's born,
> I'd take her down to New Orleans,
> And trade her off for corn.

> Bile them cabbage down boys,
> Bile them cabbage down,
> The only song that I can sing
> Is bile them cabbage down.

"Who-o-o-o whew, play it, Little Tricia," Dad would inject like he had done on the "Atkins, Travis Travelin' Show," a Grammy award-winning album.

Tricia didn't show tremendous promise of inheriting that Travis style, but to me it was the most beautiful music I'd ever heard. Our hearts were finally in harmony.

Afterwards, Tricia looked at Dad and noted, "Grandpa, you sure do play your instrument well." Dad gave the Travis chuckle I was familar with on his talk records.

There were a few more visits like this one. Sometimes Dad came to our town, Fort Worth, to play on the Johnnie High Country Music Revue at Will Rogers Memorial Center. Interestingly enough, I began working in the manager's office there shortly after our reunion. Once when I drove Dad to play on the show, my boss Mr. Magness saw me walk backstage. "What are you doing here?" he asked.

"I brought my dad to be on the show."

"Really," he responded with a strange expression. "What does he do?"

"He plays the guitar," I answered.

"Plays the guitar?" Mr. Magness asked. "What's his name?"

"Merle Travis," I told him.

Holding his cigar away from his face, he gave a big belly laugh. "Yeah, my dad's Abraham Lincoln!" he chuckled. Then he waited for my honest confession. When there was no admission of a joke, Mr. Magness said, "He really is your father?"

"Yep, he really is," I answered proudly. It was fun being Merle's girl again.

The audience loved his performance that night, and I loved him. My pounding heart nearly leaped out when Dad introduced me from the stage. "I'd like you to meet the most beautiful girl in the world, my daughter Pat and her ugly (ha) husband, Gene Eatherly." He added, "And I want to tell you I have three wonderful granddaughters, Dawn, Tricia, and . . ." He went blank. He couldn't remember our middle daughter's name. I squirmed. I felt embarrassed for him, but my heart was so full of love there was no room for anger. After what seemed like an eternity, a fan and a friend of ours, who regularly attended the show, yelled out, "Paige!"

"That's it, Paige," Dad flashed one of his big smiles. "Did you ever get stage fright?" he added, cleverly covering his blunder.

I breathed easier and found myself enjoying his show as much as any of his fans. After his performance, the crowd cheered him with a standing ovation. "That's my Dad," I responded proudly.

Finally, I thought, *the past is forgiven.* I was thankful I, too, could agree, "Feudin' Over!"

Daughter's P. S.

October 20, 1983, Merle Robert Travis died of cardiopulmonary arrest. He was residing in Tahlequah, Oklahoma, with his wife, Dorothy. At his request, his body was cremated.

October 23, 1983, several hundred people gathered for a memorial service in Ebenezer, Kentucky, in honor of Merle Travis. His famous guitar was propped against the monument which was unveiled in 1956. The sturdy limestone rock bearing the bronze plaque dedicated twenty-seven years earlier silently echoed the sentiment of the crowd. The plaque reads:

> Dedicated to Merle Travis
> who has done so much toward
> directing the spotlight on
> his home through his writing
> of folk songs about his home
> and his people . . ."

The music of Merle Travis will keep his memory alive.

Today my most cherished keepsake from my earthly father is the key he was presented to the city of Drakesboro. Upon learning of my childhood desire for this token from years past, Dad gave it to me. The key wasn't as big or shiny as I'd remembered. Actually, it was crudely carved out of wood and painted gold. But to me it is symbolic of our healed relationship. The key to all broken relationships is forgiveness and love, a lesson I had learned from my "Heavenly Father."